QUEENS
DOMAIN

MELBOURNE
(700km from Hobart)

FEDERATION
CONCERT HALL

HOTEL GRAND
CHANCELLOR

THE HENRY JONES
ART HOTEL

TAS MUSEUM
AND ART GALLERY

TASMANIAN
SCHOOL OF ART

YERS

TOWN HALL

FRANKLIN SQUARE

. DAVID'S
ATHEDRAL

MARINE BOARD
BUILDING

SULLIVANS COVE

PARLIAMENT
HOUSE

Rokeby and
Clarendon
Vale
(14km from Hobart)

SALAMANCA PL.

SALAMANCA
SQUARE

HAMPDEN RD.

BAY RD.

BATTERY
POINT

SANDY BAY

ANTARCTICA
(3440km from Hobart)

Hobart

Other titles in this series
Brisbane by Matthew Condon
Sydney by Delia Falconer
Melbourne by Sophie Cunningham
Adelaide by Kerryn Goldsworthy
Alice Springs by Eleanor Hogan
Canberra by Paul Daley

Forthcoming
Perth by David Whish-Wilson

Hobart

PETER TIMMS

NEWSOUTH

A NewSouth book

Published by
University of New South Wales Press Ltd
University of New South Wales
Sydney NSW 2052
AUSTRALIA
www.unswpress.com.au

National Library of Australia
Cataloguing-in-Publication entry
　　Author: Timms, Peter, 1948–
　　Title: Hobart / Peter Timms.
　　Edition: Updated ed.
　　ISBN:　978 1742233727 (hbk)
　　　　　 978 1742241395 (epub)
　　　　　 978 1742243856 (mobi)
　　　　　 978 1742246253 (ePDF)
　　Notes: Includes bibliographical references.
　　Subjects: Hobart (Tas.) – Social life and customs.
　　　　　　　 Hobart (Tas.) – Social conditions.
　　　　　　　 Hobart (Tas.) – Description and travel.
　　　　　　　 Hobart (Tas.) – History.
　　Dewey Number:　919.461

Design Josephine Pajor-Markus
Cover Sandy Cull, gogoGingko
Cover photograph Lisa Kuilenburg
Author photograph John Gollings
Endpaper map David Atkinson, handmademaps.com
Printer Everbest, China

This book is printed on paper using fibre supplied from plantation or sustainably managed forests.

Contents

Foreword *by Robert Dessaix*   *viii*
Author's note   *xiv*
The fabric of the city   *1*
Further afield   *28*
As seen from afar   *39*
Buying and selling   *61*
The prison becomes a salon   *93*
Doberman or labrador   *114*
A succession of pasts   *129*
Nature within cooee   *153*
'Cool off in Tasmania'   *181*
Bad behaviour   *198*
Keeping occupied   *220*
Sensory Hobart   *245*
Notes   *268*
Bibliography   *275*

... gradually it dawned on me that the voyage I needed to make began in my own neighbourhood, within a few minutes' walk of my front door. It had been there all the time, under my nose, even as I made other abortive attempts to discover a starting point.

James Attlee, *Isolarion*, p. xiv

Foreword

'Too far south for spices,' Abel Tasman wrote dismissively in 1642 on sighting the island now bearing his name, 'and too close to the rim of the earth to be inhabited by anything but freaks and monsters'. Wrong on both counts, as it happened, he sailed on rather grandly into the Pacific looking for somewhere more worth discovering. No other European bothered to put in an appearance for almost a century and a half.

All the same, as Peter Timms illustrates with abundant examples from letters, memoirs, fiction and press reports, Tasman managed to put his Dutch finger on several matters of concern to both visitors and inhabitants throughout the two centuries of European settlement. To this day many Tasmanians are uncomfortably aware of being 'too far south for spices' – that is to say, of no earthly use to anybody. The British, as we know, found a use for Tasmania as a dumping-ground for its excess prison population, but that wasn't the kind of productive use that Tasman had had in mind. With pathetic eagerness to be profitable, Tasmania has shown itself willing to chop itself down and pulp itself, if that's what it takes to be of 'use' – mainly to the Japanese, as it happens. Tasmania doesn't want to be merely beautiful. In fact, Tasmania is ready to disfigure itself in ways that will never heal, as anyone who has ventured beyond Hobart and its environs knows, if that's what it takes to prove its usefulness. Beauty is actually worth as much as or more than spices, but it takes a certain kind of maturity to understand why: richness is not the same as wealth.

At the heart of several of the pieces in the mosaic of this book, and hardly absent from any, is an echo of Tasman's second barb as well: 'too close to the rim of the earth to be inhabited by anything but freaks and monsters'. As the historian Lyndall Ryan has pointed out, Tasman probably had the fantasies of the Carthaginian navigator Hanno in mind when he wrote that – in 1642 poetry and knowledge were not quite so clearly marked off from each other as they are today – but, again, he hit on an anxiety that peppers conversations and simmers away unresolved in the minds of both inhabitants and visitors right up to the present: is Hobart too small and too far away from civilisation (Melbourne, New York, Paris — wherever you think civilisation resides) to make a civilised life possible? It's a question that people living far from their culture's metropolis have to confront all over the world, from the wastes of Siberia to provincial France, from small-town Canada to the islands of the Pacific. As we find time and again in these pages, in Hobart as everywhere else, they answer their own question with a mixture of aggressive pride in their special situation and a longing to be somewhere else — somewhere that matters. They half suspect that only 'freaks and monsters' could indeed live in their remote fastness (that in itself being a thrilling prospect for some), and half believe that they of all mankind have found paradise. It can be dizzying.

Although Abel Tasman gets a mention or two in this book, along with convicts, the odd colonial governor and some of the more colourful sides to life in Hobart in the early years, this is not a history. Given the abundance of histories of Tasmania, Peter Timms has come up with something no less useful but quite singular: a concatenation of views of Hobart. From the opinions of famous foreigners to modern-day tourists (sometimes scathing), from letters and diary entries to interviews he conducted himself with Hobart identities, he has written what is in effect a many-voiced conversation about Hobart today.

Although Peter's own voice intrudes only sporadically, it's clear, I think, that the book has grown out of a deep, although by no means uncritical, attachment to the city of Hobart. Yet, when he and I moved here from Melbourne seven or eight years ago, we did so on the spur of the moment. We'd been edging closer to the 'rim of the earth' from our starting point in Sydney's Paddington for what seemed like decades, always looking for somewhere we could have a good life without being wealthy. Eventually our gaze turned on Hobart – not in desperation, I hasten to add, although we were certainly aware it was a gamble. So we came, we saw, we bought. And suddenly, within weeks, we were living here.

It's worth emphasising that it was a move to Hobart rather than to Tasmania. There are tranquil beauty spots we could have settled in all over the country, but nowhere else that combined all the capital city amenities we craved with the pleasures of a more leisurely way of life close to nature. In other words, as Peter hints towards the end of the book, after seesawing for 200 years between forlorn, even sinister, backwater and go-ahead provincial capital, by the time we got here Hobart seemed poised to get the balance more or less right.

Remembering the old clichés about Hobart, or perhaps a school trip there in the 1960s, most people thought we were mad. A literary columnist in one of the mainland dailies, giving his readers the astonishing news that we had decamped from Melbourne, asked with a sneer if it was something they'd said. A friend in Amsterdam wrote advising us to make sure there was a hospital in Tasmania. 'What will you do there?' many asked, as if, detached from the life-support systems of Melbourne, we risked drifting off into unconsciousness, never to awake. Civilisation, they were convinced, was something you had to suffer to enjoy. After all these years, I still run into acquaintances on the mainland, especially in Sydney, who ask, completely unaware of what they're implying: 'And are you still in Hobart?' 'Yes,' I say. 'Are you still in Sydney?'

The reasons any of us feel that this place rather than that place is home have their roots deep in our own experience over a lifetime. Many years ago, for instance, in the first book I ever wrote, I described in some detail a city in a 'parallel world' I have retreated into several times a day since early childhood. Squashed between mountains and water, on the banks of a river, on an island facing south, it has all the contours of something fundamental to who I am. Not until we had actually started living in Hobart, though, not quite knowing why we were here, did it strike me that those pages in my first book, *A Mother's Disgrace*, described with almost uncanny accuracy the city outside my window.

The conversation that unfolds in this book, on subjects as disparate as the weather, the smells, the cultural life and the successes and failures of urban planning, is the kind of conversation we all have with our friends and with ourselves about the place we've chosen as home. Through the prism of Hobart, it's sure to provoke its listeners wherever they live to reflect afresh on why they've settled where they have and what 'a good life' means to them.

Robert Dessaix
Hobart

Author's note

Unless otherwise noted, all direct quotations are from interviews I conducted specifically for this book. Some people are quoted on different subjects at various points throughout so, for the sake of convenience, I usually introduce them only at their first appearance. Please refer to the alphabetical list of interviewees below if you need reminding. In most cases, I have 'tidied up' what people said, since spoken conversation, with its hesitations, grammatical slips and momentary confusions, rarely reads well when transcribed verbatim. The changes are minimal. I have been careful to maintain people's characteristic voices and, of course, the meaning of what they said.

I am very grateful to all those who gave their time to speak with me, sometimes at length in formal interviews, sometimes in passing. Several were not even aware that what they said had been noted, having been overheard in the street or in casual conversation. They remain unidentified, of course, along with one or two others who spoke on condition of anonymity.

My thanks go to the following people who agreed to be interviewed for this book:

Sohale Aftlooni *Bahai Centre of Learning*

Alison Alexander *Executive Officer, Centre for Tasmanian Historical Studies, University of Tasmania*

Max Angus *Artist*

Glen Attrill *Crew member, Aurora Australis*

Simon Barcza *Owner, Ci Simon fashion boutique*

Bill Bleathman *Director, Tasmanian Museum and Art Gallery*

Steve Bonde *Acting Assistant Commissioner, Tasmania Police*

Tim Bowden *Writer and broadcaster*

Natasha Cica *Management and Communications Consultant*

Rodney Croome *Writer and social activist*

Sarah Day *Poet*

Margaret Eldridge *Refugee advocate*

Jo Flanagan *Manager, Social Action and Research Centre, Anglicare Tasmania*

Bernard Lloyd *Author*

Dirk Meure *Former academic specialising in the administration of criminal justice*

Tim Munro *Chief Executive, Theatre Royal*

Hobart

Anne Parker *former Senior Adviser, Government House*

Amy Parkinson-Bates *General Manager, Islington Hotel*

Nicholas Parkinson-Bates *Director, Parkinson-Bates Properties*

Chris Pearce *Co-proprietor, Hobart Bookshop*

John Smith *Hobart Bellringers*

Rob Valentine *former Lord Mayor of Hobart, now a state MLC*

David Williams *Editor, Sauce*

Astrid Wright *Co-ordinator, Friends of Knocklofty Bushcare Group*

Kiros Zegeye *Community Projects Officer, Migrant Resource Centre*

Zong Xiang *Market gardener*

Tourism Tasmania did not agree to be interviewed.

The fabric of the city

In Christopher Koch's *The Boys in the Island*, Hobart is described as 'a city, but only just'. That novel is set in the 1950s and Hobart has grown a lot since then. Other capitals have grown proportionately more, however, so maybe the epithet still applies. But only just.

While, so far at least, it has been spared the worst modern urban problems (pollution, traffic gridlock, high stress levels and astronomical property prices), federalism guarantees Hobart the cultural attributes of a capital: as the seat of state government, it attracts and controls wealth and has a university, symphony orchestra, library, archive and museum along with some reasonably sophisticated leisure and entertainment facilities. Thus it is often said that Hobart is a big country town with capital-city infrastructure: the best of both worlds, manageable yet *civilised*.

It is probably fair to say that the majority of Hobart's citizens would once have leaned towards a less charitable view, suspecting that they had ended up with the worst of both worlds: the insularity of the country town with its intrinsic limits on association and choice, yet without the informal support networks or traditional forms of community they might have expected in compensation.

'We expend a large amount of money annually in advertising Tasmania as a tourist resort', complained one frustrated *Mercury* correspondent in 1938, 'and when tourists visit our shores we welcome them with closed doors and deserted streets! Wake up, Tasmania! ... or we shall certainly merit the old, jeering epithet of Slobart!'[1]

In these days of slow food, a slow city doesn't seem such a bad idea. Former disadvantages are increasingly looking like attributes, and Hobartians are casting off anxieties about their runt-of-the-litter status. After watching SBS news and seeing what is going on elsewhere in the world, they might reasonably decide that it's not so bad to be living in a little city at its southernmost extremity, in touch but out of the line of fire. People here know where they stand: they have few illusions. So while it may be more provincial than Sydney or Melbourne, you could claim, without too much of a stretch, that it is less parochial, because more outward-looking and not so self-absorbed.

Perhaps the most significant physical difference between this and other capitals is that, thanks to its size and topography, it is graspable. You can take in Hobart all at once from a number of high natural vantage points. You can see how everything fits together. 'It is not necessary to abstract a plan of its space in order to negotiate it', as the architect and planner Leigh Woolley puts it.[2]

When you do abstract a plan of it, you see that it snakes along the shores of the River Derwent, following the accessible contours. Hobart is very long and narrow: in places no more than a few blocks of suburban streets squeezed between the water and forested hillsides.

You can appreciate this best from the top of Mount Wellington. It will take you just half an hour or so by car or bus to be rewarded with a spectacular panorama stretching from the northern highlands all the way to Bruny Island in the south. Should the summit be fog-bound or the road closed by snow, you can enjoy a less awe-inspiring but more engaging view from Mount Nelson. Rosny Lookout on the Eastern Shore, although it lacks the altitude, offers the most picturesque perspective, with the city buildings reflected in the placid Derwent Estuary and the mountain rising dramatically behind. The view from the Eastern Shore has always been a favourite with artists because it can be organised into foreground, middle distance and background. The Tasmanian Museum and Art Gallery displays dozens of nineteenth-century paintings of Hobart from this side of the river, many of which exaggerate the height of the mountain for dramatic effect (as if that were necessary).

In Australia, it is not usually possible to take in a city this way, with one sweep of the eye. Other capitals are too large and lack the natural vantage points. Perth from Kings Park is probably the closest comparison.

For a bird's-eye view of Melbourne or Sydney, you must take a lift to the top of the Rialto or Sydney Tower to peer through brown haze out towards the suburbs. The customary view of Hobart, by contrast, is from outside looking in: a fairly minor difference on the face of it, but one that entirely alters your perception of the place. Seeing a city from a tall building has a definite element of triumphalism about it. It confirms the city's power and extent, and your place at the centre of it. Hobart from the mountain, in contrast, looks comfortingly toylike and vulnerable.

But not to everyone: a recent visitor from Holland, accustomed to the compactness of Amsterdam, was amazed at how vast Hobart looked from the mountain. And so it is when you consider that it supports only a little over 200 000 people. It is our love of big backyards that makes it sprawl. As early as the 1820s, less than two decades after it was founded, the diarist George Boyes noted that Hobart was spread over 'three times the space of ground' of a similarly sized English village.[3]

The surrounding hillsides mean that Hobart is a city with nowhere much to go. Although not an immediate problem to the 260-odd foreigners who set up their tents at Sullivans Cove in 1804, the steep slopes with their almost impenetrable bush would quickly prove a barrier to expansion.

One of the main things that decided them on this spot was the fresh water flowing down the rivulet off the mountain. (The Derwent is a mighty river but its navigable reaches are tidal, so fresh water was obtainable only from its tributaries.) It was, wrote surveyor George Prideaux Harris,

'… a capital spot with a fine freshwater river run-
ning into a snug bay with good anchorage & a small
Island in it, admirably calculated for Storehouse &
Battery.'[4]

To call it a river is a bit of a stretch, but nor was
it merely a creek, which, in the Australian vernacular, suggests drying up in summer. The old English
term 'rivulet', widely adopted in Tasmania, seems
just right. Harris, who dismissed Mount Wellington as 'a hill', appears to have had some trouble
with the relative scales of things. Nor, apparently,
was he thinking too far ahead, although this site
was undoubtedly preferable to Risdon Cove a few
miles upriver, where an abortive initial attempt at
settlement had been made a few months earlier.

Given that the Hobart Rivulet was so important
in sustaining the new settlers – and, of course, the
Mouheneenner people for centuries before them –
it seems extraordinary that they managed to sabo-
tage it so quickly and so comprehensively. Within
a few years Harris's 'fine freshwater river' had been
reduced to a dirty little drain, strangled by dams
and weirs upstream and lined on both sides by
windmills, factories and shanties. In 1843 it was
officially declared a sewer, accepting 'the contents
of water closets, fluids from the hospital, refuse

and dead animals, all remaining there to stagnate …'[5] While there has been a significant improvement in the water quality since then, the rivulet remains a sorry sight, at least that part of it within the city's limits.

From time to time, after heavy rain, the rivulet took its revenge by flooding low-lying parts of the city, and each time it was beaten further into submission by culverts, weirs and tunnels until eventually it was all but obliterated from the city centre. Once the settlement's lifeline – its very reason for existing – it was now a pest to be exterminated. Its treatment is depressingly emblematic of attitudes to the natural environment that have persisted in Tasmania for more than two centuries.

You can peer down on the rivulet today, skulking in its concrete culvert, from an overpass in Barrack Street. You can even enter the cavernous tunnel constraining it and walk its length beneath the city streets (although officially you are not allowed to). If claustrophobia isn't a problem, you can crawl on your belly with a torch into one of its tributary tunnels to admire the excellent convict brickwork. As you walk down Liverpool or Collins Street you can, with a little effort, still imagine yourself following the stream's lush forested valley as it rushed towards Sullivans Cove, where land reclamation has since created one of Hobart's few substantial flat areas.

So long as the tiny settlement grew naturally, it followed the line of least resistance, but the military mind of the New South Wales Governor, Lachlan Macquarie, was outraged by such chaos. During a visit to his southern outpost in 1811, he whisked up a grid plan (slightly out of alignment in grudging deference to reality), which resulted in some streets too steep for a horse and cart and others that ran straight onto the cliff-face above the beach. Yet somehow Macquarie's obdurate lay-out survived and, with much convict labour, the topography was, in time, forced to submit. Even today, however, there are streets at the western edge of the city, such as Molle, Barrack and the aptly named Hill Street, precipitous enough to terrify the learner driver.

It took a mere forty or fifty years for the struggling convict encampment to transform itself into a respectable little town, at least on the surface. By mid-century, Macquarie's grid of streets was lined with neat timber shops, although behind them were large internal courtyards where tradesmen and shop assistants lived in hovels. Historian Peter Bolger quotes an English visitor, who saw only the handsome street-frontages, as saying that, 'For a city of but fifty years growth ... none ever equalled Hobarton in beauty'.[6] No less a person than the botanist Joseph Hooker declared Hobart's shops to be every bit as good as Sydney's.

Wharves, slipways, warehouses and a smattering of small manufactories were clustered around the cove, a grubby no-go zone constantly alive with the din of heavy labour. On the surrounding low ground workmen and their families eked out their existences amid the clamour of pubs, boarding houses and brothels. Above them, on the rise, some handsome official buildings of dressed stone gloried in their own importance – buildings such as Government House, the Treasury, the courts and the offices of police – their pretensions undermined somewhat by the great grim wall of the gaol that dominated the block between Davey, Murray and Macquarie Streets. From their office windows, demure government clerks in starched white shirts and tailored waistcoats enjoyed a clear view of executed criminals swinging from the gibbets.

Commercial establishments such as banks, lawyers' chambers and office buildings clustered on the north side of Macquarie Street, while the main shopping areas were in Elizabeth Street as far as Brisbane Street and along Liverpool between Argyle and Harrington.

The best houses, impressive stone or brick structures, usually with some timber tacked on at the back out of sight, were setting the tone in New Town, Battery Point, upper Davey Street and lower Macquarie Street. A procession of more modest residences crept north over the hill, to link the city with New Town, its first satellite, as well as through the foothills west along Forest Road and along the Derwent's edge for a mile or two towards Sandy Bay.

Electric tramways – the first in the southern hemisphere – hastened the spread. The earliest lines, opened in 1893, went to Moonah to the north, Cascades to the south-west and Sandy Bay, south of the city, with later extensions to Long Beach and West Hobart. Even frequent accidents and derailments could not dent their popularity, although the press made a meal of every mishap. When little Marjorie Taylor's leg was severed in 1898, for example, a local journalist wailed tactlessly that, unless brought under control, the tramway operators 'may with impunity smash up some more Marjories and pave the line of route with amputated limbs'.[7] That must have brought great comfort to Marjorie's grieving mum and dad.

For the artist Max Angus, growing up in Battery Point in the 1920s, the tram was a ticket to freedom.

> There was almost no private transport, no-one had a car. Walking was paramount. Of course, people wanted weekends off, so they caught the tram to Sandy Bay Beach. Lord Street marked the end of the twopenny section, threepence to Sandy Bay Beach.

That was about as far as most people were prepared to venture. They remained attached to their local communities, especially those who lived out of town. In the Glenorchy district, a few miles to the north, for instance, 'there was little feeling of belonging to Hobart, a place most people rarely visited. "We didn't worry about Hobart at all" commented Mary Murdoch." Glenorchy was very much a little town on its own".[8] And the Eastern Shore hardly figured, being accessible only by punt before the construction of a floating bridge across the Derwent in 1943. Following that, the area's orchards were rapidly grubbed out for housing.

The houses of Sandy Bay, Mount Nelson, and parts of West and North Hobart and the Glebe, gaze down towards the cove, jostling for a view like spectators in a giant amphitheatre. Each generation builds higher than the last, turning suburbs such as West Hobart into architectural layer-cakes, with Georgian and Victorian on the lower slopes, Federation higher up, followed by post-war budget-moderne and finally, clinging to the topmost slopes, a smattering of showy new steel-and-glass vista-catchers.

In his essay 'Urban nature and city design', Leigh Woolley complained that planning in Hobart 'has been focused around saving areas of bush rather than defining the city'.[9] He was making a subtle but important distinction between a positive emphasis on the urban environment as a complex entity with its own internal form and logic, and a negative one that sees it merely as a sort of inexorable growth that must be kept in check.

On the contrary, says Rob Valentine, Hobart's

former lord mayor, saving these areas of bush is essential to defining the city because they are an inseparable part of it.

> One thing that really impresses me about Hobart is that when you're coming up the river, you see the foothills and they're all treed. It's a beautiful setting. Over the years they have been encroached upon, and what we need to do is to keep things at a reasonable level so we don't lose that character.

The city council's purchase of Porter Hill above Sandy Bay in 2006 was a milestone in the protection of the surrounding greenery. 'We spent millions to buy that entire hillside to save it as a nature reserve', says Rob Valentine with justifiable pride.

> It was starting to happen — development was creeping right up into that area — so council did the only thing it had the power to do, which was to buy it, with the co-operation of the owners, who priced it so we could afford it. We're trying to deal at the moment with the Hobart Rivulet, Sandy Bay and New Town Rivulets, trying to keep those avenues of green space open.

Few councils today would risk spending large amounts of public money to prevent land being built on. It is a credit to the people of Hobart that this expensive rescue mission in what is, after all, a privileged suburb, proceeded without major controversy.

Still, what does this tell us about the council's authority if this is all it can do to prevent devastation? 'The planning scheme is the law', the mayor explains:

> It controls where you can and where you can't
> develop. But where private property is concerned,
> council can't just say you are not allowed to build
> there if the scheme says you can. For example,
> there's still quite a lot of undeveloped private
> land in Lenah Valley and we could well see
> development stretching up into those hillsides
> soon and people would probably be horrified
> if that happened. But there's not a lot we can
> do about that except try to change the planning
> scheme. As soon as you do that the first thing the
> landowners would do is demand compensation,
> which they would have a perfect right to.

At least Hobart's modest, slow-growing population allows development to be kept under reasonable control. This city is not haemorrhaging in the way many others are.

That is no reason for complacency. There are those who maintain that changes to the planning scheme (or schemes, actually, because there are three) are exactly what is needed. Researchers at the University of Tasmania, for example, have declared that, 'Hobart's ability to adjust to ... economic, social and environmental changes is inhibited by outdated planning schemes that are now over 25 years old'.[10] What especially worries them is the priority given to cars. For a city of less than a quarter of a million people, Hobart has a ridiculous amount of traffic. Someone complained to the *Mercury* recently that it took him fifteen minutes to drive over the Tasman Bridge of a morning. While anyone forced to negotiate Sydney Harbour Bridge on their way to work might find that quaint, things can only get worse.

The plague of cars is partly due to the city's extent, its hilliness and its attenuated shape, which make getting around a bit of a trial, and partly a response to public transport being, well ... inadequate is the politest thing you can say about it. Without a large population to make them viable, bus services cannot attract private operators, so they have to be publicly owned and subsidised, yet at the same time there are too few people to pay for the level of subsidy required. That, at least, is the official explanation. It is also the official explanation for why a city built around one of the world's great natural harbours has no commuter ferry service. It was the official explanation for the closure of Tasmania's passenger train services in 1978 (although that also involved some federal government chicanery), and it was the official explanation for the abolition of the city's tram services in 1960.

Miraculously, though, this argument does not apply to cars. So cars rule. They have turned Macquarie and Davey Streets, often euphemistically described as the city's 'main arteries', into traffic sewers which effectively isolate the CBD from the energy and sparkle of the wharf area. Enormous swathes of land are devoted to parking, moving, maintaining and selling cars. Even the city's tourist hub around the cove is mostly bitumen carpark. Hobart's complicated system of one-way streets compounds the problem, increasing traffic volumes by ensuring that every journey involves several turns around the block, while at the same time increasing traffic speeds and throwing interstate drivers into panic.

Pedestrians hardly stand a chance. Not that they can expect much sympathy from councillors, one of whom was quick to point out, in response to the university's report, that:

> If people wish to use cars then that is a right and the purpose of local government is to satisfy people's needs, not to re-engineer their lives by refusing to provide facilities that the vast majority of people wish.[11]

Clearly he hasn't asked himself why they wish for them, or what else they might wish for if given the chance.

Although it would be fair to say that cars account for the worst of Hobart's recent disfigurements, they are not the only culprits. Like all cities of historical importance, Hobart, with more listed buildings than any other Australian capital, has become a heritage battlefield. If asked, most people today would say that the preservation of old buildings is important to them, even if they might not be able to stipulate which ones they thought worthy or why. This hardly matters, though, for they are unlikely to be asked.

At one time, not very long ago, most would have been firmly on the developers' side. In a moribund economy any new, modern building was a welcome sign of momentum. In his memoir, *Defying Grav-*

ity, Dennis Altman (now a noted political scientist living in Melbourne) remembers:

> For a long time, the head office [of Hydro Tasmania] where my father worked for fifteen years was the largest building in the state, a yellow slab at the foot of the city where a large illuminated crown, placed on top to celebrate the Coronation of 1952, was to remain for years afterwards. 'Development' and 'progress' were unproblematic for us then ...[12]

Not any more. A turning point was the construction of the Marine Board Building in 1972: a shamelessly insensitive cack-brown box plonked into the elegant old maritime quarter like some boorish bogan gate-crashing a tea party. Thirty or more years later it remains one of Hobart's most hated structures. Another is the Sheraton (now Grand Chancellor) Hotel, just up the road, built in record time in 1987 after the state government had obligingly thrown out the rule book. 'Fast tracking' is something Tasmanian governments have always been rather keen on. While the Sheraton's well-heeled guests savoured their great harbour views, for everyone on the outside the harbour had been irretrievably defaced. The hotel managed to compound the insult with its advertising, in which the building was shown from across the wharf through a forest of boat masts, as if the marina were part of its own private front yard. Such arrogance made people angry. Their city was being appropriated. Never again would a major new development proceed without public scrutiny and spirited opposition.

But does it have any effect? Sometimes it does, yes. Recently a number of insensitive development proposals have been dropped after people kicked up a fuss and the press backed them up, although, predictably, they were dismissed as 'anti-development' and 'anti-progress'. It must be admitted that such accusations, although crude, are not always unjustified: some people – often the most vocal – regard anything old as inherently good and anything new as automatically bad. Such obduracy does the cultural heritage cause no favours. The more discerning, however, recognise that the problem lies not with new buildings as such, but with the fact that almost all those we get saddled with are very *bad* buildings.

But we are not permitted to say so.

There are [explains Rob Valentine] all sorts of things in the planning scheme, in terms of the density of developments, car parking allocations,

proximity to boundaries, impacts on amenities
and so on. But when it comes to the design of
buildings, the scheme doesn't allow much leeway,
unless it's a streetscape issue or something ...
You can only have a say if it impacts on you
personally.

Which means physical impact only: if the ill-
favoured Zero Davey Street apartments reduce you
personally to tears of impotent rage, that doesn't
count. 'What's good or bad design will always be
in the eye of the beholder', the mayor adds limply.
Another alderman, Peter Sexton, is more emphatic:

> [I]t would be very dangerous and quite
> impractical to empower aldermen to determine
> both who are our finest architects and to assess
> the quality of architecture. Architects and other
> design experts rarely agree on quality, just as there
> are many different expert opinions on great works
> of art. [13]

Of course, nobody is asking aldermen to personally assess the quality of architecture. This is a
red herring, as is his reference to artworks. What
Alderman Sexton seems to be suggesting is that,
since beauty is in the eye of the beholder (which
is not in fact the case), we should just take what

we are given and shut up about it. That would certainly make life easier for alderpersons.

When they design commercial buildings, architects can rarely exercise much creative freedom. They must obey the dictates of their clients. The sheer awfulness of most of Hobart's modern city buildings is the result of developers' economic decisions, not architects' aesthetic ones. The brilliance of so much of its recent domestic architecture, on the other hand (flick through the glossy pages of *Tasmanian Life* magazine if you need confirmation) shows what can be achieved when architects are really free to exercise their imaginations and when their clients actually care about the outcome.

Councillor Sexton is mistaken to pass this off as simply a matter of personal taste. The beauty of Hobart's old buildings is a result of their consistent scale, their sympathetic detailing and the fact that they are made from local stone, timber or brick. They are all of a piece – with each other and with the landscape. In short, they are respectful of their context.

The problem with office towers in this setting is not just that technology allows them to be grossly over-scaled, but that modern transport ensures it is cheaper and easier to construct them from imported, prefabricated materials. What people love most about Hobart's old buildings is their gentle weathering. Concrete buildings don't weather. Stone matures, brick endures, but concrete just deteriorates.

Hobart is not New York, or even Sydney. It is a different kind of city altogether: essentially a horizontal, humanly scaled one. Randomly dotted about against its forested hillsides, even ten- or twelve-storey blocks are monstrous carbuncles on the face of an old friend, to borrow Prince Charles's colourful phrase.

Stand on the south-west corner of Harrington and Macquarie Streets, at the entrance to Macquarie Leisure Inn, and look up Macquarie towards the mountain. The buildings — grand old houses, most of them — are all two or three storeys high and solidly constructed of brick or stone. Their gables and chimneypots perform a lively dance along the ridgeline. Except for the tacky facade of a chemist shop and an excess of signage, their adaptation to modern commercial needs has been sensitively achieved. Each of these buildings modestly fulfils its role in a satisfying streetscape.

Now look in the other direction, down the hill toward the Town Hall. A five-storey brown box is followed by a ten-storey grey one and an eleven-storey white one, with the huge fawn bulk of Service Tasmania squatting grumpily at the end of the line. They are set at varying distances from the footpath and their tops form a jumble of discordant rectangles that obliterate the ridge-line. They throw the street below into shadow and their entrances are designed to admit giants. If the view in the other direction can be described as variations on a theme, this is a cacophony of competing blasts. The humorist Patrick Cook once brusquely dismissed this sort of thing as 'fuck-you architecture'. But Hobart is not and, provided developers can be brought under control, never will be, a fuck-you kind of town.

Of course, nobody these days expects gables and chimneypots, but nor, it would seem, are we entitled to civility, respect or a sense of ensemble. Such developments (they continue to be thrown up today all over the CBD in ever increasing numbers) make a mockery of Hobart City Council's claim that its strategic plan '... acknowledges, and is sympathetic to, the City's existing and evolving historic character and setting'[14] – although, to be fair, the council cannot always enjoy complete control.

It comes as something of a shock to discover

that in this, one of Australia's most beautiful cities, nobody in authority seems prepared to stand up and take responsibility for retaining, let alone enhancing, that beauty. The best we can do is to save isolated old buildings while desperately trying to minimise the damage caused by new ones. For example, Rob Valentine points to the ANZ building in Elizabeth Street (1968) as 'a reasonably acceptable way of developing such a precinct. It has maintained the streetscape by being set back, with a low-rise section in front, so when you walk through the bus mall you don't notice it.'

No wonder that here, as elsewhere, citizens feel increasingly locked out of the planning process. They may despair at the ruination of their city, but they feel powerless to do anything about it. While a truly concerted campaign of letter-writing or placard-waving might get a development stopped or modified, the principal players — state and city officials, property developers and banks — remain, for the most part, loftily immune to public opinion. This is not to suggest any conspiracy, only a fatal combination of self-interest, weakness and lack of imagination.

The centres of most European cities are protected by laws that ensure that new structures are in character with their surroundings. Many local councils in Britain have the power to demand that new buildings in sensitive areas be 'of outstanding architectural merit'. Some of the most innovative architecture in Britain can be found in heritage precincts: modest yet confident, scaled appropriately, respectful of its context, and distinguished by appropriate materials and finishes, all carefully stipulated in local statutes. British councils are apparently unembarrassed about enforcing aesthetic standards.

Perhaps to compensate for the insolence of Macquarie Street's office blocks and to lessen the icy downdrafts they cause, the council has planted a row of rather pathetic-looking trees in front of them. If you can't prevent ugliness, you can at least try to hide it, and a bit of greenery is the easiest and cheapest way to do so. Trees, it is said, 'soften' the built environment. Ratepayers seem to agree. When the state government asked members of the public to comment on its waterfront redevelopment plans, one said this about Mawson Place, the smart modern plaza adjacent to Constitution Dock: 'Move the sculpture, move the other unnecessary objects and make this small area into a park with a few trees and benches. This will attract people having picnics and eating chips from Flippers.'[15]

How homely this sounds. Yet that may just be the problem. The architect and planner Barrie Shelton maintains that tree-planting is a suburban, and not an urban, solution. 'In traditional hard-surface urban spaces,' he says, 'trees can quietly erode spatial integrity.' Consider, for example, the 'magnificent stone front of the Customs House ... [where] trees have been planted between the building and the water: thus, summer by summer, there are more leaves and less customs house'.[16] A bit of greenery might be helpful in hiding embarrassments, but some buildings are better left unsoftened.

We cannot entirely quarantine tourists in designated areas, however acquiescent they may be. Fortunately, though, when they do stray, they are usually more than willing to exercise selective vision — to marvel at the splendidly preserved Georgian mansions opposite Franklin Square while ignoring the gimcrack new office buildings poking up behind them, to admire the noble proportions of the old Penitentiary on the corner of Campbell and Brisbane Streets while obligingly turning their backs on the big blue Officeworks shed across the road. While this means they gain very little impression of the city as it really is, warts and all, that is not what they have paid for anyway. But for how long will they be able to ignore the inroads of the monstrous? When does Hobart the beautiful city degenerate into Hobart, the city with some beautiful old buildings?

For those who do wish to understand the true nature of Hobart — or of any other city for that matter — it is necessary to ignore institutionalised lines of demarcation and to discover those hidden underlying ones that have sprung naturally from changing histories of usage, economic conditions, population patterns, architectural styles, class differences and even subtle variations in soils and weather. They are apparent only to those who wander extensively and aimlessly, with a keen eye and an open mind. To these inquisitive ramblers the city will be revealed anew: in turn ugly, beautiful, exciting, dreary, quaint, mysterious, depressing, annoying and full of joy.

Further afield

After the Second World War, migrants arrived in Tasmania in great numbers from Italy, Greece, Poland, the Balkans, the Baltic States, Holland and, of course, Britain, attracted by employment opportunities in industries that had, in turn, been lured to Hobart by cheap hydro-electricity. It was the largest influx of new inhabitants since the convict ships and it sparked a housing crisis. In response, the state government set about constructing entire suburbs from scratch on former farming land out of town. They were planned, car-dependent neighbourhoods detached from their city centre, with water, power, sewerage and paving but little else. Inevitably, as the job opportunities dried up, they would come to be stigmatised as welfare suburbs. The attitude of the authorities seemed to be, 'give them a job, four walls and a roof, and let them do the rest'. And they did, despite the difficulties and setbacks, slowly converting paddocks full of houses into liveable suburbs.

The most ambitious of these instant suburbs was Chigwell, conceived as a model community with brick houses, schools, churches, reserves, and streets laid out in sympathy with the contours of the land. As might be expected, the reality didn't quite meet the ideal. For one thing, a post-war shortage of bricklayers meant that most of the houses had to be built of weatherboard.

These days, Chigwell looks uncannily like a low-budget Canberra, with wide, curving streets of more-or-less identical government-issue houses, lots of under-utilised open space, and a couple of forlorn shopping centres. Four-wheel-drives with bullbars and searchlights wait menacingly on nature strips and teenage girls in miniskirts wheel their babies to the shops.

Yet most of the houses are now privately owned so, although clearly underprivileged, Chigwell is dotted with pretty gardens and personalised home additions, with the occasional added storey to take full advantage of the million-dollar views of river estuary and mountains. While the housing might be a little worse for wear, the setting is beautiful and you can see how Chigwell might, in the not-too-distant future, shake off its origins and mature into a highly desirable neighbourhood.

From the end of the war until 1964, some 5000 government houses were built in the Glenorchy municipality, of which Chigwell is a part – over half its total housing stock. In all, the Housing Department put up nearly 25000 houses state-wide in the forty-five years to 1989: a huge number considering the population.[1] Many people who have spent their entire lives in Hobart's more salubrious parts without ever having ventured into the Housing Department suburbs remain blissfully ignorant of the real nature of their city. 'If I did go to Chigwell', says one, only half-jokingly, 'I wouldn't dare get out of the car'. By effectively segregating the lower classes, the government's housing policies created a huge social divide, with prejudice on both sides. Of course, all cities have their disadvantaged neighbourhoods, but only when you see at first hand their full extent around Hobart can you properly appreciate why this is Australia's poorest capital.

'What is it with people's teeth here?' asked Richard Butler, with characteristic diplomacy, on his ill-fated appointment as state governor in 2003. Tasmania then held, as it still does, the dubious distinction of having the lowest standard of oral hygiene in Australia, the unhappy result of deficient dental services. For many years it also had the highest per-capita unemployment rate, and still boasts the highest divorce rate, the lowest life expectancy, the largest proportion of unskilled jobs, the highest welfare dependency, higher rates of secondary-school dropouts, obesity and suicide, and the lowest average incomes. Statistically, Hobart does not look good.

Tourists doing the Battery Point–Sandy Bay– North Hobart–Salamanca Place circuit, where the teeth are smiley-bright, remain blissfully unaware of these problems, and even if they were, by some terrible mistake, to land up in Chigwell, Rokeby or Bridgewater, they might still not understand. These suburbs are a bit shoddy, perhaps – a bit fibro and Colorbond – but in no way could they be called slums. Hobart's poverty is mostly hidden – even more so now that, in line with contemporary thinking, the government disperses public-housing tenants among home-owners in existing suburbs.

If a drive around Chigwell helps to correct a false impression, the drive through Brighton creates one. Brighton, 28 kilometres north of the city, promotes itself as a historic town – which, strictly speaking, it is, having been settled quite early in the nineteenth century. But there is little evidence of this as you drive through en route to Launceston past service stations, fast-food outlets and vast corrugated-iron storage depots. (Pontville, an almost perfectly preserved Georgian village just up the road, is the jewelled earring dangling from Brighton's unprepossessing visage.) It is Brighton's sad fate to have grown haphazardly and too rapidly into one of those desolate semi-industrial, semi-rural fringes you can't wait to get through. Anything less like its English namesake can hardly be imagined.

Back from the main road, beyond the dusty yards of dormant semi-trailers, the scene is, in contrast, sturdily domestic. Networks of newly made streets woven, seemingly at random, across denuded hillsides, are rapidly filling with respectable brick veneers, each with its mullioned bay window, its mown lawns, a corrugated-iron shed or two and a couple of cars in the drive. Until sheltering trees get established, they bake in summer and freeze in the August gales. Since survival here without a car would be almost inconceivable, people rarely walk, making the streets eerily empty. Nonetheless, insists a local real estate agent, 'It's an ideal place to bring up a young family' and, as if to prove her point, every second backyard contains a swing and a paddle-pool. Brighton's streets are safe and quiet, the air is bracing and you can buy a decent block of land for a fraction of what it would cost closer to town. To anyone who does not aspire to the Federal Government's much-vaunted fraternity of working families, however, it looks threatening, and there can't be much for the kids to do once they become teenagers. Cultural diversity is the gift of older suburbs closer to town.

Still, whatever you might think of Brighton, it is the hub of one of Tasmania's fastest growing municipalities.

Another is Kingston, 15 kilometres out of town in the opposite direction and picturesquely separated from it by forested hills, giving it the impression of being a different city altogether (which administratively – like Brighton – it is). Kingston was once a holiday resort for Hobart folk who couldn't afford to travel far, and one or two of the original weekend shacks survive at the less fashionable end of the Esplanade. When the tortuous connecting road along the coast was circumvented by a freeway cutting straight through the hills, the area boomed. Socially, as well as geographically, it is Brighton's antithesis, boasting incomes well above the Tasmanian average, a higher percentage of home ownership, more people with tertiary degrees and more managerial and professional workers, even if most of them can't work locally and have to commute to the city. It is also the home of Hobart's Dutch community, and those who still believe in cultural stereotypes might detect something characteristically Dutch in Kingston's neat, middle-class propriety. People live here for 'the lifestyle', meaning the beaches, sports complex, golf course and two sprawling drive-in shopping malls. The dogs on Kingston's famous dog beach frolic happily in the knowledge that they have a lifestyle, and the hoons squealing their tyres outside the hamburger shop on the Esplanade are in control of (and may even be the owners of) sporty European convertibles with spoilers and mag wheels.

At the Beach Cafe Restaurant Bar, just down the road at Blackmans Bay, you can enjoy breakfast on the deck overlooking the water – perhaps sautéed Huon mushrooms with wilted baby spinach followed by maple syrup on blueberry pancakes – while eavesdropping on sophisticated young families discussing their holidays in Tuscany. The surrounding estates, with their flashy project homes, struggle to live up to the image.

To entice tourists, certain areas must be defined as special.

> Within these borders, they seem to say, people
> live lives slightly different from the norm. We
> are prepared to allow this, as long as it remains
> controllable and confined within this strictly
> defined area; if we consider it potentially
> lucrative, we might even promote it.[2]

British author James Attlee is referring to Oxford, but the observation could apply anywhere. Battery Point, with its carefully contrived mix of olde-worlde charm and smart modern living, is a perfect example of what he is talking about. To live in one of its cute Georgian stone cottages is to exist in a perpetual state of deliciously heightened reality. When street signs direct you not to the shopping centre but to 'the village', you know you're in a different realm. It is a comfort to have one section of the city set aside for the indulgence of fantasies, where people live, on our behalf, the lives we cannot lead but sometimes wish we could.

A saunter down, say, St Georges Terrace, will take you past an eclectic array of dwellings, from boxy brick walk-ups with aluminium windows to stone and timber cottages of all ages, some prettily spruced up and some forlorn. Peer over a high stone wall and you will glimpse through the trees one of the district's original sandstone farmhouses. Yet, while the whole ensemble may, in some way, evoke the past, nobody in their right mind would describe it as authentic. No nineteenth-century wharf labourer would recognise the place today. Battery Point preserves what we want while ditching what we don't, and what we want changes all the time. Today we might consider the 1960s flats overshadowing the delightfully toy-like circle of cottages known as Arthurs Circus to be a blight on its historical character that should be torn down. In fact, the whole of Battery Point would have been 1960s flats if the developers had had their way at the time. In the future, we will doubtless say the same about the sundecks and dream kitchens now being added behind Colville Street's tiny workers' cottages. We talk about preserving 'the character of the streetscape', but behind the facades modern life goes on. It is what keeps places such as this constantly in contention and prevents them from becoming museums.

Battery Point provokes envy. 'Chattering classes' and 'latte sippers' are assumed to while away their idle hours in its 'trendy' eateries. In reality, today as in the past, it is far more socially diverse than most suburbs are, with a rich mix of the wealthy and the poor, including lawyers, teachers, plumbers, builders, uni students, families, singles, gays, and old-age pensioners with cats.

Its historical character is protected by the Battery Point Planning Scheme – this is the only suburb to have one all to itself – which aims to '... allow the traditional process of gradual residential evolution and intensification to continue without allowing new forms to become dominant.'[3] In 2006, a campaign to bring Battery Point under the control of the City of Hobart Planning Scheme, on the grounds that it had no right to favoured treatment, met with spirited opposition, one resident declaring bluntly: 'The push to dismantle the Battery Point Planning Scheme is designed to open Battery Point to all the rubbish development that is allowed under the Hobart Planning Scheme'.[4]

Nevertheless, the contention in the planning scheme that council wants 'to give residential amenity the first priority', although admirable, is a little disingenuous.[5] This is no ordinary residential area, as the authorities well know, but one of those special places that James Attlee identifies. It is perpetually on exhibition. Council is anxious to keep it that way because it is proving to be very lucrative indeed. Heritage values can, it seems, be properly protected when there is an immediate financial incentive to do so.

As seen from afar

Tasmania, along with Outer Mongolia and Timbuktu, has long been a symbol of remoteness, whether of the mysterious, the enticing or the cruelly comic kind.

This was not something to bother the Aboriginal inhabitants, of course, for whom there was no other world from which to be remote. They were the centre of their own universe. Yet, although they were not aware of it, their immense distance from the centres of power was their greatest protection.

In Europe, initially high expectations of what the Great South Land might have to offer, based mostly on fantasy and wishful thinking, were dashed by Abel Tasman when he chanced upon the south coast of what he called Anthoonij van Diemens Landt in 1642. He reported 'nothing profitable, only poor, naked people walking along the beaches; without rice or many fruits, very poor and bad-tempered in many places'[1], although he had not actually bothered to go ashore. Perhaps those poor naked people on the beach, seeing the tall white sails of Tasman's ships, gained their first awe-struck intimation that some other world, hitherto unknown to them, existed somewhere far out to sea. From that moment on, Tasmania would never again be the centre of anyone's universe.

In response to Tasman's casual dismissal, the Dutch lost interest. The English, for their part, although they knew about Tasman's discovery, thought Van Diemen's Land too remote to be worth bothering with.

They changed their minds only when they realised that Australia might be more useful than they had originally thought. In 1803, Governor King in Sydney got wind of French interest in Van Diemen's Land and hurriedly sent a ragtag party of soldiers and recalcitrant convicts to plant the British flag at Risdon Cove. Its 23-year-old leader, Lieutenant John Bowen, was chosen because King could not spare anyone more experienced.

Having staked their claim, the authorities in London promptly put the struggling settlement out of their minds. It received very little attention even from the colonial authorities in Sydney, who had enough problems of their own. That Hobart survived at all was something of a miracle.

Thus a mind-set had been established: Hobart would always be the grubby little waif at the back of the class whose frantic hand-waving the teacher consistently ignored.

In light of this, it should hardly be surprising that towards mid-century, when Tasmanians were fighting for independence and the end of convict transportation, their demands were greeted by the Colonial Office with a mixture of disdain and puzzlement. To the locals, it seemed only natural that their colony should mature into a self-governing democracy, whereas in London, in Peter Bolger's colourful phrase, it was 'the cesspit of an Empire, and would always remain so'.[2]

Yet, far from trying to dispel that impression, the emancipists sought to further it. It was in their interests, as they saw it, to paint as grim a picture as possible in order to discredit the convict system. Yes, this is a horrid, gloomy place, they agreed, and it is the convict system that makes it so, offering no prospect of rehabilitation. While this may have been an effective short-term strategy, they should have known it would be counterproductive in the long run.

The emancipists' ploy was to play up the horrors of sodomy. If you put desperate men together in close confinement, they rightly pointed out, you invite unnatural practices. When the Reverend John West asked rhetorically, in execrable verse, if fair Tasmania was to be forever tainted with the name of Sodom, he was just indulging a bit of political humbug. Unfortunately, the sordid reputation stuck. Hobart was indeed estranged by the name of Sodom. Deep and abiding embarrassment about this would lead to Tasmania being the last Australian state (and one of the last places in the democratic world) to decriminalise male homosexuality, in 1997.

Violence, oppression, poverty, vice and bad weather: it was an awful lot for a small community to live down. No wonder that, when independence finally came in 1853, Vandemonians demanded the full makeover, including a name change.

It was successful, in that it helped Tasmanians to forget their past and get on with making something of themselves. But it didn't necessarily wash with the rest of the country. The mountainous island across the sea, shrouded in mist, failed to live up to that image of Australia promoted, and largely created, by the artists of the Heidelberg School and the writers of the *Bulletin:* a sunny, pastoral Australia bursting with rugged masculine optimism. There was something puny, submissive and feminised about it: something just begging for the put-down.

Thus, as the horrors of convictism faded, Tasmania, in the public's imagination, ceased to be a place of fear and loathing and became a bit of a joke. The popular image of Tasmanians as rustic and unsophisticated, which went right back to the earliest days of settlement, hardened in the late nineteenth century as the Tasmanian economy began to lag behind. An element of cruel triumphalism tainted the mainlanders' jibes. Tasmanians were to 'real Australians' as the Irish were to the British: defenceless yokels upon whom all kinds of social anxieties could be offloaded and defused. The jokes usually involved poverty and inbreeding (like the one about a Tasmanian virgin being a girl who can run faster than her brother) and they were rarely original, most of them having originated in Britain as Irish jokes, with the names changed to suit the circumstances. Even when they were funny – as the best of them were – they had about them the smell of encircling jackals.

As a rule, novelists and poets have avoided making fun of Tasmania, perhaps because that approach offers little dramatic scope. Their calumny has been of the opposite kind: that of perpetuating and reinventing the dark, violent, melancholic Van Diemen's Land of old.

Still, the island's comic possibilities have not gone entirely unnoticed by the literary world. In fact, it first appears in literature (albeit obliquely) in a political satire. Before being beached on Lilliput, Lemuel Gulliver is shipwrecked to 'the North West of Van Diemen's Land … in the latitude of 30 Degrees 2 Minutes South'. This is actually a long way from Van Diemen's Land, somewhere in the South Australian desert, but since the southern coastline of Australia had not been mapped when Swift was writing, he can be forgiven the slight.

Noël Coward cannot be forgiven his. The pompous Elyot in *Private Lives,* finding himself in an embarrassing social situation, suddenly declares, apropos of nothing, 'I once had an aunt who went to Tasmania'. The mere mention of the place was bound to get a laugh, let alone the thought that somebody's aunt was silly enough to have gone there. Coward may well have repented some years later when he came to Hobart to perform at the Theatre Royal, which he called 'a dream of a theatre'.

It was the English way to assume that any society so distant from their own civilising influence was fair game. Yet even the Americans felt they could patronise their antipodean cousins, so long as they did it light-heartedly. In the 1890s, the pioneering feminist Jessie Ackermann declared gaily that Hobart was 'delightful', with 'a complete absence of distinguished persons'.[3] To be fair, though, this was not too far off the mark and she had been no less rude about the United States.

A big city attracts famous people, repaying their attentions by cementing their celebrity. In a small city like Hobart, however, which has less to offer in the way of career advancement, the visit of someone famous is received as a sort of benediction. When Vikram Seth or Dolly Parton pop into New York, New York is doing them a favour. When they deign to come to Hobart, Hobart is flattered and grateful.

Noël Coward was just one of many forced to alter their preconceptions when faced with the reality. Mark Twain, who declared his intention to write about Australia prior to coming here, on the grounds that one always knew so much more about a place before visiting it than afterwards, was surprised to find Hobart much to his liking. As was Agatha Christie. 'It always seems odd that countries are never described to you in terms which you recognise when you get there', she noted. Hobart she found 'incredibly beautiful ... with its deep blue sea and harbour, and its flowers, trees and shrubs. I planned to come back and live there one day'.[4] Perhaps, had she done so, she might have seen, beneath the surface beauty, a suitably sombre setting for her tales of mystery and murder. That, after all, is what most writers and artists seem to have taken pleasure in revealing.

But then, that is probably what they have come looking for in the first place: the Gothick Otherland of their imagining. For them, Tasmania is not farce, as it was for Coward and Ackermann, but Shakespearian tragedy. Their darker response, based on myth and symbolism, is a literary concoction. They seek to construct Tasmania as romantic narrative.

'It looks so beautiful,' observed the poet Gwen Harwood, 'but underneath there's the whisper of death'.[5] Her view carries some weight because she lived in Hobart for many years. But it is that whis-

per of death that excites the imaginations of interstate and overseas authors today seeking a suitably
dark stage for their tales of gloom and infamy,
even those who have never visited, or have, but only
briefly. Think, for example, of Andrew Motion's
Wainewright the Poisoner, Matthew Kneale's *The English
Passengers* and Chloe Hooper's *A Child's Book of True
Crime*: dark tales of murder, genocide, religious fer-
vour and eroticism, set in a crime-ridden colonial
environment. The British-born Sydney author, Tom
Gilling, whose gothic novel *The Sooterkin* describes
a convict woman giving birth to a seal pup, set
it in Tasmania because he wanted to write about
'strangeness, alienation and curiosity'.[6]

Such typecasting can infuriate the locals. Novelist Richard Flanagan has complained, with some
justification, that Tasmania has become a quarry for
cheap exotica written by outsiders. Yet the locals,
including Flanagan himself in his first three novels,
have also been irresistibly drawn to the whisper of
death. The characters in both *Death of a River Guide*
and *The Sound of One Hand Clapping* are overwhelmed,
physically and emotionally, by the remote wilderness, and *Gould's Book of Fish* is a veritable orgy of
surreal brutality.

In an essay provocatively titled 'Isle of Gothic

Silence', published in *Island* magazine in 1994, Gregory Young outlined the history of Tasmanian *Grand Guignol*, from Marcus Clark's 1874 novel *For the Term of His Natural Life* to such works as Christopher Koch's *The Double Man*, Peter Conrad's *Down Home* and Roger Scholes' brooding film *The Tale of Ruby Rose*. Writing from his new home in Sydney, Young recalled that: 'Growing up in Hobart in the 1960s ... I thought of my island home as psychologically callous – an antipodean *Under Milk Wood*, with a nasty undertow of private belittling fanned by hypocritical public silence.'[7] His Dylan Thomas reference suggests the influence of the literary imagination.

Dennis Altman is:

> ...not convinced by the myth of Tasmanian exceptionalism. To me Tasmania represents a particular version of Australia which has failed to grow or change as fast as most of the mainland. Its conservatism is not, emphatically, the conservatism of the nouveaux riches or the ideologues of, say, Bjelke-Petersen's 'white shoe' brigade in Queensland, but rather the conservatism of an Australia shaped by a far less diverse immigrant population and a greater

sense of continuity with the past than is true for rapidly growing areas along the eastern or south-western coasts.[8]

Growing up in Devonport in the 1960s and 1970s, Rodney Croome, now one of Tasmania's most prominent social activists, always pictured Hobart as a 'distant and alien place', although, as he explains, he felt quite at ease in Melbourne and Sydney, which he had visited several times with his family:

> We used to go to the east coast and the Tasman Peninsula for holidays, which meant passing through Sorell [virtually a Hobart suburb today], and I'd beg my parents to take me into the city. They wouldn't. They said, 'There's nothing there'. I was fifteen when I first came here and then only because I was one of a group of country schoolchildren selected to greet the Queen.
>
> We [in the north of the state] were hard-working people who had earned our prosperity. Hobart produced nothing. It's the kind of un-focused resentment that was later transferred onto Canberra, particularly during the Whitlam era.

To an alert and inquisitive young man interested in history, however, this only made Hobart more intriguing. 'I became fascinated by this place that everyone hated so much. It seemed fabulous and mysterious.'

Proof of Hobart's backwardness could be seen in its buildings: those brooding grey Georgian piles that lined the city's streets; those dank little cottages with their weedy gardens and broken fences; the high retaining walls whose every mournful block of stone spoke of convict suffering. Launceston had very sensibly got rid of all that and reinvented itself as a modern red-brick metropolis, its buildings bedecked with festoons, swags and scrolls: the full panoply of late-Victorian exuberance. In his *Illustrated Guide for Visitors and Colonists* of 1885, Howard Haywood declared that, 'The people of Launceston are energetic and pushing, ready at all times to embrace new industries and carry the flag "Excelsior"!' It was a go-ahead sort of place that mocked Hobart's lethargy.

The residues of this rivalry persist to this day, sometimes in unintentionally amusing ways. For instance, a recent campaign to promote the introduction of water meters in Hobart, initiated by local business groups, thundered, 'Launceston has water meters, why is Hobart still in the Dark Ages?'

Hobartians can hardly be expected to have remained immune to the opinions of outsiders. They are acutely sensitive to what others think about them and always eager to leap to their own defence. Without the resilience of those in larger, more confident societies, they are easily wounded.

Even more wounding, however, is indifference. The sad fact is that Hobart simply doesn't register with most outsiders. Otherwise well-travelled mainlanders may never have crossed Bass Strait and see little reason to do so. If they should announce that they are moving to Hobart, the most likely response from friends will be, 'Why?' It is not the question they would be asked if they were moving to Sydney or the Gold Coast. Nicholas Parkinson-Bates, co-owner of the up-market Islington Hotel, says that promoting it in Europe or Asia is impossible without first establishing where Hobart is. 'We're constantly travelling overseas for promotional purposes,' he says, 'but we have to sell Tasmania first and then our venue. You've got to sell the state before you can sell the hotel. It's still very hard to attract the world to Tassie'.

It's the little reminders of one's insignificance that rankle: one resident says she is outraged when SBS television's national weather forecast fails to mention her home town. While not important in itself, she realises, it is symptomatic.

Hobart does not even enjoy the dominant position within the state that capitals normally assume the right to. It is not Tasmania in the way that Adelaide is South Australia or Melbourne is Victoria (at least by their own reckoning). Caravanners and motoring holidaymakers disembark the ferry at Devonport on the opposite side of the island then follow the coastline, with a day or two in the city en route. There is something about an island that makes people want to follow its edges. Those who fly in will be planning to make the city their base for day trips to the Huon, Derwent Valley or Port Arthur. Even tourists pouring off cruise liners at Sullivans Cove are loaded onto waiting buses and whisked out of town. Hobart seems destined to be a transit point. 'One of Hobart's great advantages', claims the Lonely Planet Guide, with unintentional irony, 'is its proximity to some of the best scenery and most popular sites in the state. Getting out of the city takes no time at all ...'[9] This is reminiscent of Barry Humphries' wisecrack that England is a wonderful jumping-off point for the Continent.

However, insignificance, while it may be hard on the collective ego, does offer advantages to some.

Film star Merle Oberon used it very effectively when she claimed to be Tasmanian to cover up the awful truth that she was Indian, which, in a race-obsessed Hollywood, might have ended her career. Tasmania, she rightly assumed, was so far away and unknowable that nobody was likely to challenge her. And nor did they, least of all Tasmanians themselves, who were quite flattered to have sired a film star.

Errol Flynn, on the other hand, was the genuine article. His father had been a professor of biology at the University of Tasmania. On arriving in Hollywood, he pretended to be Irish, because he wanted to put his unhappy past behind him and because it was easier than constantly having to explain where Hobart was. He changed his mind when he realised that coming from an unknown place made him all the more exotic and mysterious. It certainly worked for Merle. In 2008, Flynn's daughter, Rory, visited Hobart from Los Angeles to film a television advertisement and 'to make up for' her father's neglect of his birthplace. 'What really surprises me', she said, 'is that dad never came back, it really surprises me'.[10] It shouldn't have. Clearly Flynn had outgrown his humble birthplace. Ambitious people usually do.

One annoying thing about coming from a place that nobody has ever heard of is the likelihood of its being mistaken for somewhere else, somewhere perhaps a little better known with a similar-sounding name. It can lead to awkward social situations. Hobart poet Vivian Smith was asked in Switzerland if rhinoceroses were a problem in Tasmania. Later, in England's Lake District, he was complimented on his command of the language: 'One would think English was your native tongue', he was told admiringly.[11]

Perhaps these awkward situations would not arise if Tasmanians abroad, when asked where they came from, simply said 'Australia', as travellers from other states do, instead of insisting on being *Tasmanian.* But while 'Australia' has now lost whatever mystery it once held for foreigners, 'Tasmania', which does not conform to the sun, surf and sand image, retains its exoticism. In a world becoming progressively more uniform, that is something worth exploiting.

Today the tables have been turned completely. Neither abhorrent nor the butt of jokes, Tasmania has been reinvented as a peaceful, urbane refuge from a world gone mad: a place to escape to rather than to escape from. The historian Alison Alexander says:

When I first went to the mainland when I was about fifteen, I noticed that people felt sorry for me coming from Tasmania and they'd speak a bit slowly and enunciate carefully. That was the case until about 2000, when suddenly it was good to be Tasmanian, with the food and wine being so good, and the environment pure and so on. Almost overnight those perceptions changed.

Even the old gothic literary tropes can lead to happy outcomes. *The Last Confession of Alexander Pearce* is a classic — some might say clichéd — filmic exercise in the Tasmanian *Grand Guignol* tradition: a grisly, true tale of escaped convicts eating one another during a terrifying bid for freedom. Yet it apparently created a surge of interested enquiries from potential tourists and sea-changers when it screened on the ABC early in 2009. These people, seduced by the spectacular scenery, apparently saw murder and cannibalism as no impediment, so long as there was no chance that they would be personally affected, of course.

'When we went to the interview with the Australian people,' recalls a West African woman of her first contact with immigration officials at a refugee camp,

> ...they said Australia is a good country and
> everybody is friendly, and that is all. So we didn't
> know if it is cold or if it is hot and we didn't
> know we were coming to Tasmania. ... We thought
> we were going to Sydney or Melbourne. But when
> we arrived in Sydney they said we have to catch
> one more aeroplane. We knew it was Hobart but
> we thought Hobart was a suburb in Sydney. We
> saw lots of bush and we thought oh no they are
> just going to throw us down there and it was scary.
> When we came here nobody speaks our language
> and we thought oh no, it is the end of the world.
> You better trust me, it was not easy. It was scary.[12]

To a Melbournian or a Sydneysider accustomed to the cultural diversity of Springvale or Cabramatta, Hobart's homogeneity will be surprising, even a little dismaying. 'It looks awfully Anglo', as one visitor noted disparagingly. And it's true, Hobart is awfully Anglo, but not because of any inbuilt prejudice or resistance. Tasmania has a very good record of accommodating overseas immigrants, although it has not always been adept at keeping them.

Even the earliest settlers were a surprisingly diverse lot. The convicts that David Collins brought to the Derwent in 1804 — who would become the city's founders — included a Pole, a German, a Portuguese, an African American, a Frenchman and a couple of Jews from the East End of London, among the English, Irish and Welsh.[13] Later, Pacific Islanders, black Americans, and men from the Azores, Cape Verde Islands and the West Indies would join crews hunting whales off the south coast.

Following independence, Tasmania lured thousands of sturdy British labourers in the hope that they would teach the ex-convicts a thing or two about discipline and manners. In theory, none were more suited to that task than the German Lutherans, who began arriving in the 1870s, the first non-British immigrants to come in any numbers. Unfortunately, they kept pretty much to themselves, settling in a remote valley behind Glenorchy, so their impeccable moral example was somewhat lost on the locals. There, after years of extraordinary hardship and deprivation, they established a town they called Bismarck (tactfully changed to Collinsvale during the First World War), with a school, a general store and churches. Collinsvale is not much changed today, with the same rarefied air of rural remoteness, despite being only thirty minutes from the city centre.

Like the West African woman quoted above, Europeans who came here after the Second World War had little choice about where they would end up. Unlike their British counterparts, assisted migrants had to work for two years wherever they were sent. Consequently, many left when their time was up and their skills were less in demand. Frankly, there were easier places to live in the 1950s and 1960s if you were Polish, Dutch or Serb.

Those who stayed helped to rejuvenate the state's economy. The claim has often been made that they also transformed Hobart's staid, insular society into today's outgoing one, with its 'vibrant artistic community and its burgeoning coffee culture'.[14] The first things anyone mentions when you ask them about the benefits of multiculturalism are food and coffee. After that, they tend to run out of ideas. Yet perhaps food and coffee are enough: Hobart's array of Italian, Japanese, Chinese, Vietnamese, Greek, Indian and Middle Eastern eateries, and of course its innumerable cafes, are enough to convince most people.

Yet, although creative and energetic individuals

from Europe and elsewhere have made great contributions to Hobart's cultural and social life – one who springs immediately to mind is the winemaker, industrialist, arts entrepreneur and environmentalist Claudio Alcorso – it is a big step to then claim that immigration has been responsible for transforming Tasmania's post-war society. Migrants have simply been too few, their communities too small, and their prospects too limited.

Many of those who came for economic reasons, whether willingly or otherwise, have drifted away again. Those who stay very often do so for reasons that have nothing to do with financial security: the friendliness of the locals, the slow pace, the natural environment and the climate are their priorities, and they are prepared to make economic sacrifices for such intangibles.

Kiros Zegeye, who arrived here with his wife and family from northern Ethiopia about three years ago, is well aware that in Melbourne or Sydney they could be enjoying better job prospects and the company of their compatriots. However, unlike most refugees, Kiros was able to choose where he settled and he chose Hobart: 'I liked the topography and the climate, which reminded me of home... the natural environment here is beautiful.'

Refugees from Bosnia who arrived here after the Balkans war also found comfort in the terrain and the crisp winters, until unemployment and the need to be part of a bigger Bosnian community forced most of them to leave. It would be nice to think that today, on the hot, flat plains of Melbourne's outer west, there are Bosnians pining for Mount Wellington just as much as for the mountains of their original homeland.

Buying and selling

It has long been a sore point with those in the rest of Tasmania that Hobart, as the administrative centre, soaked up wealth rather than generating it. The view from Launceston, in particular, was of a capital full of pollies and bureaucrats feeding off the fat of the land, a prejudice that to this day feeds the rivalry between north and south.

It *is* a prejudice, to be sure, although not an entirely baseless one. To a greater extent than its counterparts on the mainland, Hobart, which has never been a major source of capital, has had to draw its sustenance from outside.

This gives rise to one of the qualities that visitors notice most about this city: its curious atmosphere of being marooned, with no visible means of support. As one young man asked in a loud American twang outside a Salamanca bar, 'What the hell keeps this place going?'

Well, these days, for better or worse, he and his friends do. But to answer his question properly, we need to go back a bit.

The infant colony suckled directly from the teat of the Mother Country. The convict system might have been morally repugnant, but it was a nice little earner and, when transportation ended in 1853, Hobart lost not only its free workforce but also some generous British government subsidies. Freedom had its price. To make matters worse, wheat, wool and whales – the colony's main staples – declined in value over the following decade, through a combination of diseases, competition from the mainland and, in the case of whales, sheer greed and carelessness.

According to an irate journalist in 1841, the discharge of whale oil from boats tied up at New Wharf (opposite Salamanca Place) was 'disgusting to the eye and offensive to the nose'.[1] But it smelled sweet enough to those making a fortune from it, and that money flowed through to the rest of the tiny community. Although whales had already been eliminated from the Derwent Estuary by this time, Hobart remained the centre of operations for the southern whaling industry. According to historian Michael Nash:

> From 1827, when reliable statistics become available, until the demise of whaling in 1900 the exports of oil and bone out of Tasmania totalled over £2,700,000 in value. At the peak of the industry between 1837 and 1841 they were worth over £530,000.[2]

That was a lot of money, and the slow decline of whaling from the 1840s onwards was a major blow that exposed the colony's unstable financial base.

Economically speaking, Tasmania's problem – in the past as now – was its small population. For one thing, it meant the government did not have a big enough tax base and, for another, the market could not sustain local industries. It was far cheaper to import manufactured goods than to make them. Tasmania seemed destined to ship out raw materials then buy back the goods that other countries had made from them, which is bad for both economic stability and collective self-esteem. Although some Huon Valley fruit, for example, was processed in Hobart (almost everyone over a certain age can recall the pungent smell of hot jam that filled the air around the wharves), the vast majority of it was packed for export. The local IXL brand was famous throughout the colonies and overseas, but only British jams were acceptable to the genteel classes.

When, in 1871, the discovery of a mountain of tin set off a mining boom on the west coast, the direct benefits flowed to ports in the north, which revealed another problem for Hobart: it was in the wrong place. This only made the good folk of Launceston cockier. Hobart was, in fact, doing rather well for itself by this time. Largely by virtue of being the administrative centre, it remained the colony's busiest port and this, along with the continuing opening up of the hinterland, guaranteed work for city businesses. Wages were not so bad, people's diets had improved, and they enjoyed a wide range of sporting and cultural facilities. As far as uncharitable northerners were concerned, however, such good fortune was unearned and undeserved. This was in line with a common nineteenth-century belief that the only legitimate economic activity was one that resulted in the production of tangible things (a mindset that some Tasmanians have found very difficult to shake off). Some in Launceston even had the temerity to suggest that *their* city be made the capital, knowing full well that this would have reduced Hobart to almost total irrelevancy.

The sudden and dramatic collapse of the Bank of Van Diemen's Land in August 1891 (partly as a result of a fall in world mineral prices) was a psychological disaster as well as a financial one, plunging people into unemployment and destroying public confidence. Not only was Hobart too isolated and too small, it was too poor as well. The best and brightest left in droves and recovery would take generations. Yet even a depression can have its positive side, and from this one would emerge three hidden benefits: tighter government control of the economy; increased support for Federation, which, it was realised, would effectively compel the wealthier states to subsidise poorer ones like Tasmania instead of crippling them with trade tariffs as they had been doing; and the growth of trade unions.

> As the depression of the 1890s locked the
> community in a colder grasp [writes Peter Bolger],
> the have-nots realised once more that, as in the
> convict days, the 'people' were dispossessed by
> their fellow men within their own city. A problem
> for the future was to be that of inequality of

wealth as that of the past had been inequality of opportunity.[3]

Except insofar as it revived the state's economy overall, a second mining boom in the early years of last century proved to be of no more direct benefit to the capital than the first. Instead, it turned Zeehan, a little mining camp on the west coast, into Tasmania's third-largest town, with seventeen pubs, a theatre of noble proportions and its own newspaper. Civilised folk in the capital could only look on with a mixture of horror at the upstart's Wild West lawlessness and a certain grudging admiration for its enterprise, from which they looked forward to being subsidiary beneficiaries. Indeed, so they became, at least for a while, until the bubble burst. By the early 1920s the profits had vanished and Zeehan was practically a ghost town. There followed another depression, then another world war. The blows just kept coming. (In actuality, the wars benefited the state's economy by pushing up demand for minerals, but you can run an economy on supplying armaments manufacture only if you are powerful enough to keep the wars coming.)

Ups and downs, booms and busts: something had to be done to stabilise the state's economy.

The government had little option but to encourage manufacturing industry, yet what incentives could it offer? Inexpensive electricity, generated by the abundant waters of the highland lakes, was clearly the one to go for. With the Hydro Electric Purchase Act of 1914, the state-owned Hydro Electric Department came into being. From then until the decisive Gordon-below-Franklin dispute in the 1980s, no wild river would be safe from its ravenous appetites.

Some twenty-six years after its founding, the Hydro-Electric Commission, as it was now known, could boast in its first report to parliament:

> ... Tasmania is not a thickly populated state, and
> to embark on such a national scheme represents
> a great Governmental experiment, and, though
> it has had many critics in the past, it must be
> admitted today that it is performing a paramount
> service; it has brought Tasmania to the fore as an
> electrical State ... [4]

Soon after Hobart was connected in 1915, Cadbury chocolates became an early catch. It was a good one, too: henceforth generations of Australian mums and dads, if they thought about Hobart at all, would think 'Cadbury' and when they visited

Hobart a tour of the factory was high on their lists of priorities. Other interstate companies followed, Comalco being one of the more prominent, in 1955. By the late 1960s, 'Electric Eric' (as premier Eric Reece was called) could boast that Tasmania's economy had never looked better, and his enthusiasm was infectious. 'Our school history was of Hydro power and progress', recalls Stephen Alomes. 'That Bell Bay [aluminium smelter near Launceston] used more power than the whole of Western Australia was an item of pride to school-teachers and students in the early 1960s.'[5]

However, by the time the High Court of Australia at last put an end to the Commission's grandiose plan to flood the Gordon River in 1983, cheaper and more diversified power sources were already attracting industry to other states. The Hydro era was waning, although the Commission, which had grown into the state's most powerful political lobby, would not concede without a fight.

Not for the first time, Tasmania had put all its economic eggs in one basket and suffered the consequences. In his *Van Diemonian Essays*, Peter Hay complains that:

> We yearn for more people, and for the whopper
> industry that will, in one stroke, guarantee

perpetual economic prosperity. We dream of a
crane and smokestack future that the rest of the
world is already seeking to put behind it.[6]

In the 1980s the Liberal government of the aptly
named Robin Gray, so obstinate and unregener-
ated in other respects, had had the sense to realise
that the state's economic future lay not (or at least
not only) in the whopper industry but in small to
medium-sized businesses, especially those based
on tourism. Catamaran-builder Incat (founded in
1978) was one company that reaped the benefits,
reviving a tradition of ship-building in Hobart that
went right back to the beginning of settlement. So,
although the 1990s' recession was tougher on Tasmania than on the rest of the country, recovery was
quick and decisive. The early years of the present
century, under Labor premier Jim Bacon, saw the
economy stronger and more diversified than ever,
despite the continuing dominance of the woodchipping industry which had taken over from the
Hydro as the state's principal political powerbroker.

Tourism is hardly new to Tasmania. It was
already a significant contributor to the local economy by the end of the nineteenth century. However, only after air travel had become safe and cheap

would it start to be exploited with gusto. Discount airfares have delivered Hobart its latest windfall.

Which brings us back to our American friend sipping his beer in the Salamanca sunshine.

What draws him and countless others are Tasmania's forests, mountains and wild coastlines, the very assets that other money-making enterprises have been so carelessly sacrificing. With touching irony, the Tasmanian tourism industry is now exploiting the past glories and terrible environmental legacy of the once mighty west-coast mining industry. The poisoned King River near Strahan and the denuded Queenstown hills are impossible to avoid, but they can be turned into object lessons about the blunders of previous generations. Such melancholy spectacles add gravitas to one's delightful holiday experience, topping it off with a touch of hubris – look how much better we do things today! Forestry, however, which does not appear to be doing things better, is more difficult to memorialise. Forestry Tasmania, a state government-owned company, is valiantly having a go but its myth-making will strike all but the most gullible as mere dissembling. Tourists, who come to have their fantasies confirmed, are put off by too much unpleasant reality.

While they come for the scenery, they are increasingly being urged to linger in town by a melange of festivals, restaurants, bars, historical buildings and, latterly, voguish art. Hobart, or at least those parts of it that tourists are expected to see – has spruced itself up, or 'rebranded', as they say. 'MONA FOMA [Museum of Old and New Art Festival of Music and Art], a new urban festival of music and art, is determined to turn Hobart into a musical and visual dreamland where anything can happen', according to the tenaciously hip programme for the city's latest bash. Some even talk hopefully of an 'arts-led' economy. The dowdy old maid is being reborn as a trendy chick, although it's clearly a bit of an uphill battle. Both state government and city council are chipping in with cosmetic improvements to paving, lighting and signage that they were reluctant to bestow on mere residents in the past.

While visitors can be relied upon as a major source of wealth, the locals' pockets have been picked no less assiduously over the years. Premier Edward Braddon was the first to realise their potential, choosing the depths of the 1890s depression to exploit the poor and vulnerable with a Suppression of Public Gaming and Betting Act, whose stated aim was to minimise the really dangerous forms of gambling. What it meant, in practice, was that, instead of betting happily amongst themselves, people would have to direct their money into George Adams's Tattersall's Sweeps lottery, from which the government could take its cut. Tatts would be run nationally from Hobart until its move to Melbourne in 1956.

It was only appropriate that the city that had given Australia its national lottery should also have been first with a legal casino. Wrest Point, opened with great fanfare in February 1973, was expected to attract thousands of cashed-up interstate visitors. And so it did, until overtaken by more salubrious gaming houses in other states. For one brief shining moment, Wrest Point gave Hobart a thin patina of sparkling sophistication, as the only Tasmanian hotel with 24-hour room service, professional entertainment, sporting facilities and quality restaurants.

Today's patrons cheerfully subvert the image. There seems little point in dressing up just to play the pokies and watch footy on a flat-screen tele.

Strapless evening gowns and dinner jackets are far less in evidence than jeans, cotton print frocks and trainers without socks. Few even pretend any more that gambling is glamorous or sophisticated, and those who do just look as though they're trying too hard. The staff, immaculately groomed, with fastidious manners, must wonder why they bother.

It is perhaps significant that, while Tasmania trails behind the other states in so many other respects (health care and education spring to mind), it has been something of a trendsetter in the liberalisation of gambling laws. Whether it be horse racing, sports betting, casinos, keno, footy pools or church-hall bingo nights, we've generally lighted the way. Easily our favourite methods of getting fleeced, however, are lotteries and the pokies. There are 3680 electronic gaming machines in the state, into which Tasmanians pour around $130 million each year.[7] All are controlled by Federal Hotels Group, which enjoys the exclusive right to operate gaming tables, pokies and keno throughout the state. Federal is almost impossible to avoid, being the owner of two casinos, many hotels and clubs, several major tourist facilities and a lot else besides. It is one of just a handful of major players who dominate the state's economy.

They, at least, are doing very well out of gambling. The state government is too, enjoying an annual tax-take of more than $80 million. True, this is a regressive tax, in that, proportionately, the lower people's incomes the more they tend to pay, but let's not quibble over details: the state's economy must surely be benefiting overall.

A report commissioned in 2008 by the Department of Treasury and Finance suggests otherwise. It found that the gambling industry did not contribute significantly to the financial wellbeing of the state, and had virtually no effect on tourism, investment, or employment. The government's tax revenue is, after all, coming from taxpayer's pockets and going around in circles.

Yet, contrary to popular opinion, Tasmanians appear not to be all that heavily addicted. On average, they each gamble $774 a year, which is modest when seen against the national average. Sadly, though, this does not mean Tasmanians are more sensible than mainlanders, just less cashed-up.

It is the social cost of gambling that worries most people. That cannot be calculated, although the report has a go, suggesting something in the order of $90 million a year, which represents a lot of broken families, clinical depressions and attempted suicides.

Not many visitors notice it, or at least can put their finger on what it is. Of course, the old buildings are attractive, you are never too far from a decent cappuccino, and complete strangers say hello to you in the street. But there's something else, something more fundamental, that lends Hobart its charm: or, more specifically, the absence of something.

From the moment you get off a plane in Melbourne or Sydney you are bombarded with opportunities to part with your money. Every wall, every street, every tram or bus, every park bench is desperate to sell you something: cajoling, enticing, seducing and bullying. There's a free offer, an irresistible bargain, a lifetime guarantee whichever way you turn. This lends big wealthy cities their atmosphere of perpetual, if superficial, excitement. Hobart, in contrast, has room for some public space that is not for sale. Advertising exists, of course, but it is less muscular, less dogmatic, less intimidating. Hobart is surely Australia's most under-branded capital city.

Not that anyone planned it this way. As with so many of the city's most appealing attributes, the paucity of global mega-brands is the natural outcome of penury and a small population. Hobart simply isn't big or wealthy enough to excite their interest. While this clearly has its disadvantages, at least it leaves people free to go about their lives without feeling constantly harassed. As a result, they are not so likely to see themselves one-dimensionally as consumers, which, in turn, makes them reassuringly uncompetitive and non-aggressive. Hobartians are less concerned with buying 'lifestyles' than with just getting on with their lives.

This happy situation may not last. The lifestyle-mongers are gathering. One by one, the city's buses are morphing into moving billboards. Economically and socially, Hobart is getting bigger, richer, more cosmopolitan and ambitious, but also harder, more alienating and materialistic.

For the time being, however, it remains a city of small shops. Just before the Second World War, recalls Vivian Smith,

> …there were tobacco shops and barbers, hat makers and curio shops, not to mention all the second hand clothes and furniture and book shops that flourished in Liverpool Street; and I knew children at school who lived above shops in Murray, Macquarie, Elizabeth and Melville

Streets, shops that were demolished to make way
for petrol stations and department stores.[8]

The focus of his pessimism may have been the
Myer Emporium, which had taken over Brownells
Bros in 1959 and quickly expanded into the Johnston and Miller building in Murray Street, almost
overnight becoming the largest department store in
Tasmania. Conservative Hobart shoppers could be
forgiven their concerns when, just a few years later,
Myer combined with the other major department
stores, FitzGeralds and Charles Davis, to develop
a smart new shopping arcade on the site of the
old Cat and Fiddle Tavern, right in the centre of
town. It didn't help, of course, that Myer was a
Melbourne firm – a foreigner, and a rich and powerful one at that. This looked suspiciously like
colonisation. As it happened, however, Hobartians took the newcomer to their hearts. It would
become the city's main drawcard, the mother hen
around which Hobart's smaller shops clung for
protection and support. So much so, in fact, that
when Myer's historic Liverpool Street building was
destroyed by a spectacular fire in 2007, there were
public outpourings of sorrow and dire predictions
about the ruination of the city's retail economy.

Far from starving Hobart's small shops, Myer had given them a new lease on life.

Today they survive in great numbers, not yet banished to the suburbs by exorbitant rents and multi-storey developments. Since minimal capital is needed, small shops are constantly appearing, flourishing, failing, changing hands or remodelling. There are, for example, an extraordinary number of jewellers, with half a dozen in Liverpool Street alone. Fone Zone ('SMS, Facebook, MySpace and More') sits happily alongside the Resource Collectables recycling shop, whose windows are a muddle of old encyclopedias, 1960s Mixmasters and mounted beer coasters. Elderly clockmakers hunch over cluttered workbenches in laneways next to sandwich shops where unnaturally cheerful women in aprons make to order. Just up the road, Routleys displays Italian business suits and elegant silk scarves for the young businessman with an eye to promotion. It is the small shops, old or new, smart or down-at-heel, that shape the character of the streets: modest, domestic and manageable. This is a wonderful city for strolling, a city that rewards the window-shopper with a rich variety of experiences.

While strolling, you might pop into Kafé Kara in Liverpool Street for a short macchiato and a

Monte Carlo. Or, for the same money, the CWA shop around the corner in Elizabeth Street will sell you an iced rainbow cake big enough to feed the family for a week. The girl at Kafé Kara, in jeans and tee-shirt, calls 'Hi there' as you enter, while the coiffured ladies at the CWA will murmur a polite 'Good morning'. Leave your socks and, for a small sum, they will darn the holes for you. New Hobart and old Hobart, happily thriving side by side, at least for now.

A lot of books are sold here: perhaps more per capita than in any other Australian city. Yet the market is too small to interest the global chains, so independents still have the field more or less to themselves. The two main bookshops, Fullers in Collins Street and Hobart Bookshop in Salamanca Square, are more than holding their own against online booksellers because their book launches, poetry readings, discussion groups and friendly personal service have nurtured loyal followings. Literate Hobartians tend to be either Fullers people or Hobart Bookshop people, and they can expect to be greeted by name whenever they visit.

As a child in the late 1950s, Chris Pearce hung around his father's bookshop in Collins Street, absorbing the trade that would become his life:

Fullers opened just after the war in 1946. It
wasn't the only bookshop in the city when I was
a boy. There was OBM, which is now Angus &
Robertson, and Ellison Hawker. Both have been
there a long time in their original positions.
In those days ninety per cent of books were
hardcovers and my father kept an amazing stock.
He had every James Joyce in hardcover. He said he
could sell one *Finnegans Wake* each year, and he was
thrilled by the look on people's faces when they
found it. He had a policy of not throwing out or
returning any Penguins he ordered and he kept
to this right up until the seventies, so when we
moved the shop to Murray Street we took a huge
stock of late-fifties' Penguins, still priced
at 2/6d.

Fullers is now back in Collins Street, owned by
Clive Tilsley, while Chris runs Hobart Bookshop
in Salamanca Square with partner Janet Grecian.

There's been a dramatic increase in book sales
over the last ten or fifteen years [says Chris].
Since we moved to Salamanca, about half our
sales in the summer months are to tourists.
They're fascinated by Tasmania, so we sell lots of
Tasmanian books to tourists, as well as popular

novels, which are also what people want when
they're on holidays.

Yet a reliance on tourism can be a mixed blessing:

> After the Martin Bryant thing happened [the
> shootings at Port Arthur in 1996] there was a
> dramatic drop in tourists coming into the shop.
> We really noticed it. The other time was when the
> shop was in Liverpool Street and the first Gulf
> War started. The tourists just stopped coming.

One urbane Melbournian, visiting the Theatre
Royal for *West Side Story*, was condescendingly
amused by some slightly overdressed young women
in the foyer organising their social calendars around
the start of lambing season: 'No, not the week of
the 15th, I'm needed on the farm'. This is nothing
for the locals to be embarrassed about. Hobart is
enriched by its living roots in the countryside. The
CWA shop is but one small reminder. Another can
be found just behind the Theatre Royal, amidst the
fashionable apartments of the Wapping district
(notorious in the nineteenth century for its vice and
prostitution but now a smart place to reside). The
cavernous interior of Roberts Limited is stacked
with stock feeds, horse drenches, fencing wire,
hay bales and mysterious implements that only a

farmer could have any knowledge of. Although it has not entirely resisted gentrification, with space increasingly given over to gardening supplies, on any Saturday morning its carpark will still be dotted with dusty utes with brown dogs and shovels in the back.

There is a reassuring continuity in this continual small-scale process of adaptation to fashion and circumstance. When developers show up, however, with their big plans and big money, that continuity is severed for ever and some essential source of cultural nourishment withers. Social values specific to this particular place are swept away by anonymous commercial ones that belong everywhere and nowhere.

A poignant example is the plan by Melbourne developers Riverlea Australia for an 'innovative, bold and purposeful' new office tower on the corner of Liverpool and Murray Streets, which has dislodged the Flower Room, a cut-flower and produce co-op run by volunteers. The Flower Room's co-ordinator, Pat Newlands, pointed out that they had been trading for sixty-six years. 'We have nowhere else to go and have always been a city-based business', she told the *Mercury*.[9] That's all very well, but in the innovative, bold, purposeful new Hobart, that is not what cultural heritage means.

Eventually, inevitably, Roberts will move further out where land is cheaper and the dusty utes don't have as far to come, and the CWA will close its city shop. New Hobart is swallowing up old Hobart at an ever-increasing rate. This is a city in transition.

But transition to what? Where is it all heading? For one possible answer, we must go to the outskirts.

Out-of-town shopping malls are common to almost all modern cities, of course, but their economic impact will inevitably be greatest on smaller, poorer populations and their aesthetic impact is all the more brutal when they are dumped onto a peaceful semi-rural community. Cambridge Park Homemaker Centre, on the road to Hobart Airport, is a generic example of the species. There is little point in describing its sprawling agglomeration of merchandise-laden hangars, since everyone from Dallas to Beijing has seen their own more-or-less identical version. Cambridge Park has the weedy trees wedged between the parking bays, the obligatory public sculpture, the same extravagant ranges of pasta-makers, lounge suites, patio settings and wading pools, and the same grim-faced young

Ashlees and Jedds meandering listlessly from Harvey Norman to Bennetts to Sleepy's looking for ways to max out their credit cards.

The faltering economy has put a nearby 'big box' shopping development on hold for the time being but, if and when it gets up, these two together will increase the total retail space in Greater Hobart by nearly a third. Can they survive? More to the point, can Hobart's central business district survive?

'Well, at this point it's difficult to say', begins Rob Valentine, cautiously.

> If you add thirty per cent more retail space
> to the entire Hobart area in one hit, by our
> estimates it will take eighteen years to absorb
> that increase because people don't have thirty
> per cent extra spending money. We don't have
> the population levels. So what happens? For
> one thing, you're spreading your workforce
> over a thinner area. People say they're great
> for employment but how many jobs have
> been created? These places require far fewer
> employees than would be needed in town. The
> customer gets a lower level of service across
> the board because they're taking the workforce
> out of the CBD ... Retailers in the city don't

mind competition but the big-box development at the airport will be on Commonwealth land, so it's exempt from the normal planning procedures. It's not a level playing field. And the infrastructure is not in place: for example, there are no public transport services, so the city's resources get stretched even further. The central city concentrates resources, making it cheaper and more efficient to provide them. These big developments on the fringes are not good land-use planning.

He has reason to be negative, because such developments are beyond council's control and therefore its rate-collecting reach. Others are more sanguine. In order to compete, they say, the central city might have to specialise and gentrify, which might help to lift it out of its torpor.

While the mega-mall makes no bones about its single-minded determination to flog as much stuff as possible, Salamanca Market, its ideological opposite, is selling something intangible: *authenticity*. Or at least a pretty good simulation of it.

'Set between graceful plane trees and the mellow sandstone facades of historic warehouses,' croons the council's website,

Hobart's famous market at Salamanca Place attracts thousands of locals and visitors, every Saturday of the year. They come for the food and music, fresh fruit, crisp organic vegetables, hot baked spuds, the warm aroma of a coffee and croissant, busker's singing the blues ... They come for breakfast, scrambled eggs and orange juice at a Salamanca bistro, then a stroll along the hundreds of stalls, meeting friendly people who make or grow what they sell.[10]

As the flurry of adjectives suggests, this is less about shopping than adopting a lifestyle, one in which trees are always graceful, stone invariably mellow, and where unfailingly friendly people never walk but stroll.

In truth, Salamanca Market, a retail franchise owned and run by the city council, conforms to a global stereotype almost as rigidly as the Cambridge Park Centre does, albeit with very different results. There are street markets like this all over the world, organised on the same principle, selling local handicrafts, fresh produce and imported knick-knacks, and catering to a standard mix of tourists and locals.

This is the sort of cultural heritage that *is* welcome in the new Hobart: the sort that can be managed and marketed. Salamanca market is emblematic of Hobart's romanticised self-image and, as such, the fulcrum around which the city's tourism industry turns.

Nevertheless, while it may be no less an artificial construct, the market acknowledges, as Cambridge Park does not, that there is more to life than the dogged amassing of things. It turns shopping from a competitive into a co-operative experience. Rows of tightly packed stalls, each laboriously set up anew every Saturday morning, stretch from the silos at the foot of Battery Point, past Parliament House Lawns and up the hill to Davey Street, where they meet the edge of the city proper. On a sunny summer's day you can hardly move. Here, cut flowers, woolly jumpers, beanies and second-hand books; there fruit leathers, fudge, hotdogs and 'the smallest pancakes in Hobart'. A little further on, potato peelers, jams, honey, leather purses, belts and wallets. The buskers, the spruikers, the pamphleteers, the general atmosphere of mild mayhem, all confirm this as a public event in public space where variety and a degree of freedom are cheerfully encouraged. In stark contrast, the private owners of shopping malls impose rigid controls that disallow any behaviour that will not contribute to profit-taking.

But one cannot live on atmosphere alone. There's the larder to be stocked. And while the fresh organic produce at the market is worth elbowing your way through the crowds for, at some point you're bound to decide that it's easier just to pop down to the corner shop, especially as Hobart does corner shops better than any other city in Australia.

Aware of the problem, the city council did what municipal authorities always do in the circumstances: it hired a consultant to write a report, the Salamanca Market Sustainability Study, which confirmed that locals are visiting the market less often than they used to because it is too crowded, parking is difficult and the fresh fruit and vegetables that were once so abundant are giving way to jewellery, trinkets and novelties.

> [T]here are warning signs [the report says] that
> the Market is becoming tired and in need of
> being taken to the next step. In marketing terms
> it can be said to be at the 'mature' stage of the
> product life cycle and may be entering or about to
> enter the 'decline' stage.[11]

One wonders what they might have said about all those French provincial markets that have been thriving since Medieval times.

'The next step', apparently, will be through a maze of strategies, target segmentations, stake-holder-group studies and methodologies. The report even commends the 'strategic objectives ... that Shopping Centre property managers have'. In short, a more commercial orientation and more bureaucratic control. This will strike those outside the closed circle of management-speak as entirely counter-intuitive.

People go to the market for the experience, not the shopping. It's fun. But it's not the sort of fun you want every weekend. Salamanca has none of the easygoing atmosphere of street markets in Europe or Asia. You can't really browse; you can't pause to indulge in a bit of friendly bargaining; and, despite the council's encouragement, you can't really stroll. It's all much too frantic for that. Nor is there any-thing like the range of local produce you would find in a traditional market overseas or, for that matter, at Melbourne's immensely popular Victoria Market: no meats, no fresh fish and few dairy prod-ucts. Plucked ducks do not hang in rows; no eels or crabs wiggle in tubs; cheeses are not stacked in end-less variety, begging to be sampled. What produce there is has to be searched for amidst the welter of copper bracelets, leather jerkins and tee-shirts.

The one part of the market that really works for the locals – the part that is meant for serious shopping – is the so-called Hmong Alley. These are people who have, after all, been doing markets for generations.

In the 1970s, the Hmong, originally from Laos, began arriving here from refugee camps in northern Thailand. Many settled in Moonah, where landlords who couldn't afford to be fussy were prepared to tolerate Asians, and where large backyards allowed them to do what they did best: growing fruit and vegetables. Later, they established market gardens on the city's outskirts. Their section of the market, a cornucopia of tomatoes, bok choy, crisp spring onions, carrots, asparagus and fat white Chinese cabbages, organically produced and picked only hours beforehand, was once a much larger component of the market than it is today.

By the turn of the century, many of Hobart's Hmong had gone to seek their fortunes on the sugarcane fields of North Queensland, although a few have since returned, defeated by the humidity and disillusioned about the fortunes. One is Zong Xiang who, with her aunt and another woman, farms three large blocks at Richmond, supplying the gloriously fecund Hill Street Store and Best

Fresh Wholesalers in Patrick Street as well as her own market stall. 'We work hard,' she says, 'and I have to get up at 5am to get the market stall set up. It takes about two hours. But I make a good living and the children are happy.'

The energy and purpose the Hmong have injected into Salamanca Market is not the result of any strategy or rebranding exercise. It was one of those things that just happened, through a fortuitous combination of historical events: a simple matter of supply and demand. Perhaps this is why the summary of conclusions in the council report fails to mention them.

If you want to spot the locals at the market, look for those battling a little tetchily through the crowd with beetroot, rhubarb and celery spilling from the top of their carry-bags. Were the market able to meet more of their weekly requirements, so that they didn't have to then troop off somewhere else to get the rest, there would doubtless be a lot more of them.

While Salamanca Market may not differ much from its counterparts elsewhere, it is special in the particular relationship it enjoys with its host city. Hobart is just the right size, has just the right population mix, and is close enough to its agricultural areas, to make it a perfect market town. Salamanca Market represents an ideal of the sort of small, localised commerce that many see as the future for compact cities that want to trade on their difference. In commercial terms, it has a symbolic importance that far outweighs its actual financial contribution, significant though that is.

The prison becomes a salon

An important rite of passage for children comes at that moment when they are first made aware of the world beyond. Then the intimate world they have been inhabiting up to that point shrinks and along with it their whole sense of self. For the young Peter Conrad it was a pineapple that did it, bought by his parents at a Saturday-morning market.

> It was an object of wonder to me [he recalls], a taste from beyond ... Everything had to travel so far to get to us that the most ordinary items – that supernatural fruit; English magazines, three months out-of-date when they arrived – had an aura because of the distances they had crossed.[1]

The pineapple that so captured the boy's imagination was, his parents told him, imported, which meant 'from the mainland'.

Christopher Koch writes of his fictionalised alter-ego, Francis Cullen:

> He lived in an island. At six years old, after he had started school, Francis knew about that. He knew it because people talked about the Mainland: there was an island because there was a Mainland, where he might some day go, when he grew up.[2]

Living on an island did, on the other hand, give children from better-off families one claim to worldliness over their mainland counterparts: they were more likely to have flown. Dennis Altman, the son of solid middle-class Jewish parents, became accustomed to flying from an early age because it was:

> … the most practical way to reach Melbourne for our annual holidays. I remember the excitement when the old DC3s gave way to the new 'turboprop' Vickers Viscount, the sense of sophistication involved in crossing Bass Strait for Melbourne.[3]

Now that crossing Bass Strait is routine, and primary-school kids are likely to know their way around Barcelona, perhaps they are robbed of an important rite of passage as a result. Yet despite the disillusioning effects of mass transit and mass media, they may still experience that moment when the awesome reality of being *peripheral* suddenly hits home.

At any social gathering in this city, the conversation will quickly turn to some delightful *pensione* in Italy, taxi fares in Phuket, or the joys of falling into the gutter at Oktoberfest. While physically they are in Hobart, in their minds people are somewhere else. If this is true everywhere, it is more true here. Those who live on the edges direct their gaze toward the centres. 'Exodus', as Syd Harrex once observed, 'is of special significance to islanders.'[4]

'Right on the wharves,' remembers Vivian Smith of his pre-war childhood, 'or in the streets nearby, various shipping firms had their agencies, with bright posters inviting one to see various parts of the world ... The port brought intimations of the excitement and allure of overseas, of foreign places.'[5] Today, visiting cruise liners have resurrected some of that excitement, more because of their intrinsic glamour and immensity than where they might be headed. Otherwise, travel has become a drearily familiar round of check-ins, security scans and baggage allowances. Most people would consider it a sacrifice worth making.

One former resident claims that the only thing that kept him sane when he lived here was the open-dated airline ticket waiting in his office drawer (a small psychological prop denied to the disgruntled now that airlines no longer issue tickets). For such people, the outside world offers legitimation and adventure. It is, by definition, more interesting, more exciting and more sympathetic than anything Hobart could possibly have to offer.

The pull towards the outside is counterbalanced by a pull towards inwardness and a defensive self-satisfaction: 'we're fine as we are and if you don't like it you should go somewhere else'. This can lead to a debilitating aversion to criticism and debate, sapping the city's intellectual vitality. The challenge is to be able to appreciate the possibilities in each, to avoid the pitfalls of both, and to come to some kind of accommodation that is not predicated on concerns about whether somewhere else might be better or worse.

In the nineteenth century, people were not accustomed to moving far from home. Before they embarked (willingly or otherwise) on the long voyage out to Australia, most free settlers and convicts had never ventured beyond the village they had been born in. Once they arrived here, they were unlikely to have had either the incentive or the opportunity to leave, since even the trip to Sydney was expensive and hazardous. As long as Hobart remained prosperous and, along with Sydney, one of the country's main centres of population, there was no reason not to stay and make a go of it.

England would always be 'Home' nonetheless, even for those who knew they would never return, and for their children who had never actually been there. England provided an anchoring point for a society that felt itself adrift. As the visiting author Anthony Trollope noted in the 1870s, 'Everything in Tasmania is more English than is England herself ... The Tasmanians in their loyalty are almost English-mad'. Tasmania, he wrote, wanted to be thought of by Great Britain 'as a child that is loved'.[6] He was right to an extent, and he nicely captures the obsequiousness involved, although Trollope encountered Hobart only through its governing classes: those most insecure and anxious to kowtow.

They inscribed themselves upon this unfamiliar, unconducive space by overlaying it with memories, gestures and customs. They filled the void with names, by which they possessed, domesticated and, in their own peculiar way, honoured their wild new abode.

In his book, *Van Diemen's Land*, James Boyce points out that Tasmania's reputation as a Little England was, to a degree, fabricated, largely by that master of image-making, Governor Lachlan Macquarie, during visits to his southern outpost in 1811 and 1821. His aim was to remake the new land in the image of the old. In this he was remarkably successful. Names were his tools.

As expressions of colonial deference, Elizabeth, Victoria, Liverpool and Warwick Streets are unexceptional. But there are street signs in Hobart to make even the staunchest Anglophile blush: Paternoster Row off Warwick Street, for example (which, if you half close your eyes, does actually look the part), or Britannia Place and Pembroke Place in Bellerive.

The Duke of Wellington, at the height of his powers when Hobart's expansion began, is ubiquitous: his namesake mountain glowers down over all; Salamanca Place commemorates one of his victories; North Hobart's Wellington Street is among thirteen around the state that bear his name; and Duke of Wellington Hotels are everywhere. A lovely conglomeration of scrambled allusions in Battery Point sees Waterloo Crescent, Cromwell Street and St Georges Terrace plunging down-hill into Napoleon Street. Perhaps the insult was intended, perhaps not.

'Hobart' itself will strike most of us today, if we step aside from its comfortable familiarity, as singularly inappropriate. Lord Hobart, Secretary of State for the Colonies, was hardly an important enough figure to warrant the honour. Commander David Collins, the man charged with setting up the colony at Sullivans Cove, was just trying to ingrati-ate himself with the boss. Sullivan was even less deserving, being Lord Hobart's undersecretary.

A few folksy alternatives to these official desig-nations survive as reminders that ordinary people did not always fall into line, least of all the native-born, who, by the 1840s, were leading the push for independence from Britain. There is a Chimney Pot Hill Road at Ridgeway and, somewhat con-frontingly, a Niggers Lane in Kingston (although that might be more recent). Billy Goat Lane and Nanny Goat Lane in Battery Point – so named, presumably, because only goats could conquer their steepness – are wryly amusing, a point that today's authorities, with an eye to the tourists, have hammered home with quaint olde-worlde sign-posts. In general, however, vernacular names are blandly descriptive: Old Farm Road, Beach Road, Old Coach Road, Hill Street and so on. Sometimes they continued to be used even after an official Anglophile name had been conferred. Not many of them survive in the city and suburbs, where the officials did their job thoroughly, although they are relatively common in the countryside: a road cutting called Black Charlies Opening is still proudly signposted on the east coast, providing much amusement to travellers.

According to the *Companion to Tasmanian History*, the area now occupied by Hobart was originally called Lebralawaggena, which is colourful, although not exactly catchy. The original Palawa (Tasmanian Aboriginal) place names were largely ignored by both the authorities and their subjects. Curiously, however – perversely even – there was a fashion in the early 1900s for Maori words.

Aboriginal terms are still notable for their absence from Hobart's geography today, Moonah and Lenah Valley being rare exceptions. In the 1950s – the era of pokerwork boomerangs and Corroboree-pattern Laminex – some effort was made at redress, with indigenous words being co-opted for streets in Chigwell and some of the other new suburbs. They no doubt had a ring of fashionable sophistication about them at the time. Geilston Bay, Kingston Beach and Howrah throw up the occasional Nayuka Street, Wombara Avenue or Mookara Street amidst the Sovereigns, Stratfords and Dovers, but they are not specifically Tasmanian.

The paucity of indigenous place names might well be just a result of nobody having bothered to record them or, given their sometimes tongue-twisting complexity, nobody being able to pro-nounce them. In any case, as Greg Lehman has pointed out, the local tribes often used different names for the one place, depending on the season, the time of day, or the context in which it was being talked about, and that doesn't really work for a street sign.

From the onset of hard times in 1840 until the mineral boom of the 1870s, the lure of the out-side world became an imperative for many young single men who had given up trying to find employ-ment at home. Many more fled the city to work in rural areas. James Boyce reckons that 'About 8,000

people, mainly former convicts, left Van Diemen's Land in the three years from 1847 to 1850 alone, and the large majority went to Port Phillip', although the exodus was partly offset by immigration.[7]

It is a problem that dogged the state until very recently. In the late 1980s, Neil Batt, leader of the Labor state opposition, declared it 'an economic disaster'[8] that, on average, sixty-one people were leaving the state every week. The exodus barely countered the natural growth rate, leaving the state's population virtually static at about 448 000. As a consequence, school populations declined, government services and infrastructure stagnated, and taxes imposed on those who remained were increased.

Those with ambitions to be artists or writers departed because they lacked intellectual stimulation, and because they could not expect to make a name for themselves on the periphery. They had to live where they would be seen by those who mattered, to wangle their way into the cliques and institutions where reputations were made. For the moderately ambitious, Melbourne or Sydney would suffice, but the holy grail was success in London. The sculptor Oliffe Richmond was one of the few Tasmanian artists to achieve it, in the

1960s, but only after he had studied in Sydney and been awarded a New South Wales Travelling Art Scholarship.

Would he have succeeded had he stayed in Hobart to study? Perhaps not. As late as 1961, students at the art school were still following a syllabus laid down in the 1890s.[9] Picasso, the Surrealists, Expressionism, abstraction: it was as if they had never happened. Those lucky enough to get a place at an interstate or overseas college must have got an awful shock when they arrived and realised how far they lagged behind the other students.

Then suddenly, in 1986, when the School of Art completed its move to a converted jam factory in Hunter Street, it was catapulted from near-oblivion into acknowledged status as the best tertiary art school in Australia (the best tertiary art school premises, that is). Tasmanian artists and writers today are not compelled to leave in order to succeed. They still have to make a splash in the centres of influence but, thanks to modern communications and transport, they can do it from a distance, without having to fully immerse themselves. They can be peripherally in the thick of things, using their relationship to the major centres as a form of creative exploitation.

There is something typically Tasmanian about the art school's sudden, unexpected change of circumstances, something perhaps characteristic of fringe societies in general: they tend not to adapt gradually. Change in response to outside influences will be stubbornly resisted until it no longer can be, then it is as if a dam has burst. When they feel they've been left behind, people act boldly to prove themselves to the rest of the world: 'We'll show you we're not as reactionary as you thought!' Consider, for example, how the most repressive homosexual laws in Australia changed overnight into some of the world's most liberal; how, after generations of untrammelled environmental destruction, Tasmania produced both the world's first green political party and Permaculture, a radical system of agriculture; how the state with the worst record of violence towards indigenous peoples became the first one to grant financial recompense to victims of the Stolen Generation; or how works of startling originality such as Richard Flanagan's *Gould's Book of Fish* and innovative arts companies such as the avant-garde opera company IHOS have burst from the belly of a hitherto timid arts culture. Entrenched conservatism gives the creative something solid to kick against.

Robin Boyd, writing in *The Australian* in 1969, conceded that:

> Australia's greatest contribution to world civilisation may begin, when it comes, in Adelaide or Hobart or Ballarat or any of a score of smaller towns. Yet, to be realistic, it is more likely to begin in a place where there are enough minds rubbing against each other to send off a few sparks. It seems to be necessary to build up a pressure from two or three million people to eject one or two such sparks.[10]

Although this seems reasonable enough in theory, history does not entirely bear him out. Florence in 1400, at the dawn of the Renaissance, had about 60 000 people, a little less than a third of the population of Hobart today, which did nothing to inhibit its great contribution to world civilisation. A large number of people might allow for more creative and intellectual activity but that activity will not necessarily be innovative. A plethora of competing interest groups, the great weight of bureaucracy, and the sheer expense of getting anything done, mean that big centres are accustomed to playing safe. They are more concerned with protecting their own power and privilege. Fringe societies, on the other hand, can afford to take risks because they have less to lose. They don't always seize their opportunities – in fact, fearful of how others might judge them, they are too often content to follow blindly – but when they do, the results can be startling.

Hence, cities such as Hobart are a strange mixture of the deeply conservative and the fearlessly innovative, with a relative lack of middle ground.

Until very recently, it would have been fair to say that the deeply conservative had the upper hand. They enjoyed most of the power and controlled most of the finance. Therefore, they largely determined the public outlook. Thanks almost entirely to MONA, that balance has tipped.

The secret of MONA's startling success lies not just in its flare, its daring and its ambition. After all, art museums the world over, from Bilbao Guggenheim to Tate Modern, can make similar claims. The added ingredient in MONA (or the Museum of Old and New Art, as it is almost never called) is the irresistible myth in which it comes wrapped: a delicious fairy tale about a disadvantaged working-class boy from Glenorchy, 'internal to the point of autism', as he himself puts it, who drops out of university, discovers a magic formula for generating money from horse-racing and instantly emerges a multi-millionaire. He happily spends his fortune on a vast underground pleasure palace filled with fantastic treasures and – in the final note of grace – invites everyone in to share his triumph. Who could resist?

And, like all good fairy tales, this one has an underlying element of darkness, which manifests itself in the building's architecture and the choice of exhibits.

On entering a modest pavilion at ground level (there is, perhaps, some symbolic significance in the fact that it is a converted family home), we descend, like Alice, through a hole in the floor, finally emerging, wide-eyed, into a vast rock-walled cavern. From there, we will quickly lose ourselves in a maze of underground chambers, some tiny, some stupendously large, where Egyptian sarcophagi, Pacific bark cloths, African masks and Roman coins rub shoulders with paintings, photographs and multi-screen video installations. Anselm Kiefer, Damien Hirst, Andy Warhol, Giacometti, Sidney Nolan, Kandinsky: there is a surprise around every corner. Although far from being a random assemblage, the thematic categorisations conform to no patterns we recognise. In the exhibition, *Theatre of the World*, for example, which opened in mid 2012, one room was devoted to human dismemberment, another to grids, another to the eye. Despite the razzmatazz and playfulness, however, more than one visitor has been thoroughly spooked by the experience.

But whether you love it or hate it (it's bound to be one or the other), your over-riding impression is likely to be awe, not just at its size and the vast expenditure lavished upon it (anything from $100 million to $200 million, depending on who you ask), but at the realisation that this is one individual's personal indulgence. In contrast to other major museums, MONA is not an institution. It has no board of management and the curators are not answerable to any bureaucracy. Which is one reason people, especially Tasmanians, have taken it so readily to their hearts. They do not go to MONA to be educated, but to have fun, to be stimulated and awaken their senses. Blissfully indifferent to hierarchies of value or the conventions of art history, or to arcane absorption in matters of taste, MONA invites us to share in a lively, occasionally crazy, conversation, rather than submit ourselves to a lecture. Which makes it the most liberating of museums.

It helps that David Walsh, the super-rich man in question, is the very antithesis of the classic museum benefactor: an unlikely working-class hero, self-deprecating, capricious, dismissive of intellectual posturing and notoriously uncouth. Many museums trade on the eccentricities of their directors but few can claim directors as flamboyantly eccentric as this one. He is, in fact, a serious man of sharp intellect, but he is careful not to let on.

The first thing people will tell you about MONA is that, since it opened with great fanfare in January 2011, it has quickly become Tasmania's premier tourist attraction. Even the state's tourism authorities, baffled at first that a contemporary art museum should have proved such a drawcard, have belatedly got on board with special MONA package deals. Although the state government played no part in MONA's establishment, it has belatedly woken up to the fact that the arts might be a nice little earner. However, the financial benefits, although of course welcome, are, in the end, something of a distraction.

MONA has done a lot more than just rescue a flagging tourism economy. It has changed the city's body language, teaching it to stand up straight and look others squarely in the eye, even putting a swagger in its step. Used to being a follower of inter-state and overseas trends, constantly looking over its shoulder to see if it was measuring up to what others were doing, Hobart suddenly finds itself a trend-setter. Far more than merely demonstrating that the arts can pull crowds, MONA has created an atmosphere, even amongst those not especially interested in cultural pursuits, in which culture seems to matter, as if part of the city's underlying character.

As a result, some major arts projects have been given renewed impetus. For example, the University of Tasmania and the Tasmanian Government have committed funding for a new Academy of Creative Industries and Performing Arts, including a new Conservatorium and recital hall, to be built next to the Theatre Royal. And stage one of the Tasmanian Museum and Art Gallery's long-awaited refurbishment is now well under way, with far more likelihood of continued government support.

The new TMAG promises to be MONA's perfect complement, and quite unlike any other state museum. For one thing, it will be housed in a suite of historical and contemporary structures (including the Bond Store, Australia's oldest public building) that in themselves will form a museum

of Australian architecture. As befits such decon-
structed premises, the museum's multifarious col-
lections of art, natural and social history, science
and anthropology will be mixed and matched so as
to bring the various disciplines into a lively debate.
Furthermore, those aspects of the old museum
that many locals, perversely perhaps, found most
endearing, such as its rabbit-warren complexity and
its rather eighteenth-century cabinet-of-curiosities
multiplicity, will be replicated and reinterpreted
using new technologies: a sort of museum of the
museum. In short, the reborn TMAG promises to
'blurr the boundaries' in an adventurous and distinctive way that would simply not be possible for
major state institutions in Melbourne, Sydney or
Brisbane, with their established hierarchical structures and jealously guarded curatorial divisions.
The question of whether it will be as *good* as they
are – a question that would previously have been on
everyone's lips – simply won't arise because com-
parisons of that sort will be meaningless.

What has brought Hobart into the world's conversation as never before is globalisation, making
the city more open to ideas, more diverse and more
tolerant than it was in the past, and increasingly a
player in world events. Yet, at the same time, glo-

balisation is exerting a constricting influence. Those who refer to it as 'Americanisation' have a point. It increases the demand to measure up against centralised notions of success, making eccentricity and singularity – those engaging qualities of the marginalised – increasingly difficult to sustain.

For the present, society here is poised tantalisingly between one world and another, enjoying the benefits of regionalism and globalism in roughly equal measure, each happily being milked to complement the other.

At nineteen, Natasha Cica could hardly wait to get out of Hobart. 'I felt I knew everyone. I felt stifled. I wanted to make my own way somewhere else.' Now, twenty years later, having lived in Sydney, London and elsewhere, she has returned to run her own management and communications consultancy. 'I came back', she says,

> … because instead of seeing the smallness of
> the community here as a prison, I now see it as
> a salon. This is very attractive to me, and the
> mix of professional and creative activities I'm
> involved in is more possible here than it would
> be in other parts of Australia, partly because of
> the scale of things. It's easier here to connect with

like-minded people, especially across disciplines, so the circle of people I mix with includes not just other writers but visual artists, performers, business people and lots of others. That's quite special to this place.

What transformed the prison into a salon? A change in her own needs and expectations, for one thing, but also an improvement in Tasmania's economy and social prospects that has seen many interesting, creative people move here from interstate. Importantly, she can 'fly to the mainland to gain a different perspective', and communicate instantly via email and the internet. Living in Hobart, she says, 'you're not completely off the map as you were twenty years ago, but you're still separate enough. There's a wonderful freedom that comes from being off the mainstream's radar'.

Doberman or labrador

Despite MONA's considerable impact, nobody would call Hobart a glamorous city. There are no glittering Hermès or Louis Vuitton stores. The central business district is brick and plaster, not marble and stainless steel. To be frank, it is a little dowdy — 'snug and eventless', as Christopher Koch once put it — like a country town that never quite shrugged off its origins. The visitor will be charmed rather than excited. Not that this is necessarily a bad thing, of course: you can find glitz and razzle-dazzle almost anywhere these days, but charm is rarer. It is also a lot more difficult to get right.

As for the streets, so for the people in them. The stylish young things in Hilfiger and Bally who smile out from advertising posters upon Hobart's grey cardies and Gore-Tex look as though they've washed up on the wrong shore. People might primp and preen for afternoon tea at Government House or a gala night at the Theatre Royal; and restaurants such as Garagistes and Ethos are setting new standards of sophistication, but in the streets the drab and down-market rule. 'I've never seen so many badly dressed people', one visitor exclaimed. Is this a sign of poverty or what comedian Lennie Bruce once called 'poverty-envy'? A bit of both, perhaps. As the old joke goes, everyone knows everyone anyway, so what would be the point of putting on airs?

The weather works against sartorial dash. These days, unfortunately, glamour is usually confused with sexiness, in the young, pouty, half-naked sense, and you can't achieve that when you're wrapped in winter woollies. All the same, Londoners, New Yorkers and Parisians maintain their suave image (at least the ones who can afford to), despite those cities being far colder than Hobart.

One difference is that Londoners, New Yorkers and Parisians have efficient, heated public transport to whisk them to and from work, and arcades and awnings to give them shelter. Hobart, in contrast, is a very exposed city, making it pleasant in warm weather but heavy going when cold winds bring rain down off the mountain. Those who walk or cycle to work – and they are many, given that, apart from cars, few practical alternatives are on offer – have reason to be grateful for their Gore-Tex and beanies.

Just as importantly, though, London, New York and Paris are big, cut-throat and anonymous. Creating an image works only when others are either unaware of the real you or don't give a jot, because they are busily putting on airs of their own. Keeping up appearances is important in a competitive environment, but much less so in a small one, where personal grooming, beyond a certain point, might come across as trying too hard. If any image can be said to prevail, it is the rugged outdoorsy one which, although not exactly haute couture, establishes one as a dependable, bush-walking, salt-of-the-earth type. Hobart has a remarkable number of hiking-gear shops, all of which appear to be doing considerably better than the high-fashion boutiques.

For the sake of egalitarianism, Hobart's rich prefer to keep a low profile. When multi-millionaire David Walsh appears in public to promote his new Museum of Old and New Art, he does so in old jeans and tee-shirt, which say, 'I'm just an ordinary bloke like you.' It's not true, of course, but it is important that he claims it is.

This was not always the case. In the early nineteenth century, when convicts and ex-convicts made up a large proportion of the population, the visible signs of social status mattered a great deal. The rich and powerful – government officials, military officers and the few well-off free settlers – got about in expensive British-made clothing, while the rest had to satisfy themselves with kangaroo-skin jackets and other locally made garments. Being seen to be of a high social class was essential. Hobart was a snobbish society.

Despite, or because of, hard economic times at the close of the nineteenth century, keeping up appearances remained a preoccupation of anyone who wanted to be thought of as decent. The honestly toiling middle classes aspired only to staying warm and protecting their modesty. 'Clothes for girls were thick and heavy,' writes Alison Alexander,

> …and underclothes included flannel petticoats, flannelette drawers and woollen stockings knitted by their mothers. Even on a hot summer's day these stockings were not taken off. In winter

girls wore thick jumpers and skirts, with rubber galoshes and buttoned gaiters over their legs.[1]

Clearly glamour was not a priority, although special occasions called for something pretty. It was only when girls started going to work in the city that their personal appearance began to be a daily concern to them, and only then could they afford to buy nice things.

Coats were the big sellers. In the 1930s Connors in Harrington Street was advertising 'Girls' and maids' Tweed Coats, fully lined, dark fawn shades, 13/11d each'. If that was a bit below your station, McLow's in Liverpool Street might tempt you with their 'Canadian skunk-collared coats in green, brown, rust, navy and black, reduced to 59/6d'.[2]

Improvements to the heating of buildings and new lightweight synthetic fabrics spawned a greater range of choices after the war, although the shops were not catching on quickly enough for some. One disgruntled fellow complained in 1963 about the men's undergarments in city shops: 'I am astounded at the carpet-like fabrics of which they are constructed – ghastly relics of a cloistered and stuffy Victorianism.'[3]

Rules of etiquette, which elevated the genteel

above the common herd, were rigidly enforced. Margaret Eldridge, a teacher from London, arrived in 1964 after her husband had secured a posting at the university. 'I'd done a little research', she remembers, 'but I really had no idea where I was going.' She was shocked to find that ladies always wore hats and gloves when going to town. 'I was stared at for wearing slacks in public.'

Margaret Scott, who would go on to become one of Tasmania's best-known poets, came out from England at around the same time. 'When I tried to start my own little network', she later wrote, 'nothing went right'.

> I couldn't speak the language. I asked people to
> tea and they turned up at six o'clock expecting
> a baked dinner only to find withered cucumber
> sandwiches and coffee cake that had been drying
> out since four. I didn't understand that in
> Australia in 1960 clothes and money mattered
> more than accent.[4]

Things are different today. According to Simon Barcza, the owner of Ci Simon boutique in Hunter Street, 'people's priorities are for cars, holidays, good meals in restaurants and nice homes. Clothing tends to be a low priority.' Over his twenty or more years in fashion retailing, he has noticed a sharp falling-off of interest. 'People were much more stylish ten years ago than they are now. They spent more on clothing and they dressed better. Today they go for cheaper things.' Yet he doesn't believe Hobart is unique in this respect:

> The same is true in Sydney and Milan. Hobart is a micro-economic measure of the rest of the country. The range of income levels is much the same. It's just that with such a small population you're more likely to notice the differences.

The trend, he says, is towards lighter clothing. This reflects a generational change: young men, for example, don't wear coats as their fathers almost always did. 'In the eighties a rack of over-coats would sell in a week. Now you couldn't give them away.' He puts this down to a warmer climate and, more plausibly, to efficient heating in buildings and cars: today we are just better insulated in other ways, and have the benefit of weightless synthetic paddings. For young males, under-dressing is a source of pride. Getting around in a tee-shirt when the frost is thick on the ground is an indicator of virility.

Nicholas and Amy Parkinson-Bates, who work

at the 'high end' of the tourism industry, with business interests around the world, are more sceptical. In Sydney and parts of Melbourne, says Nicholas,

> ...everyone's looking pretty flash. People make more of an effort there. You see people in Hobart and you think, 'Yeah, he's put some effort into what he's wearing, but it's just not stylish.' They've put thought into the way they dress but they don't so often make it work. We both find it very hard to go shopping in Hobart.

Despite lip-service being paid to 'buy local' campaigns, which do their best to promote state loyalty, many women still make a point of flying to Melbourne or Sydney to shop.

> We know people who look gorgeous [says Amy], and we ask where do you go shopping and they say Sydney or Melbourne. So there's a market here, but obviously not a big enough one or we'd have more retailers of high-end fashion.

Obviously bigger cities offer greater choice, but there is also status in being able to say you bought your new outfit interstate (or, better still, overseas). In any case, if you purchase it locally your friends might know how much it cost. It is a good idea to pretend it was bought in Melbourne or Sydney even when it wasn't, both to maintain your pride and hide the price.

Nicholas believes Hobart is ready for a precinct of high-class boutiques and designer shops. 'It's a golden opportunity for a creative developer. I think the art movement that's getting established here will help develop fashion consciousness. The two go hand in hand.'

It is an eternal hope, and a vain one, that somehow the city can be transformed by sheer force of will against its very nature. People want to mould it into what they think it ought to be, while retaining all those aspects of it they want retained, which they fondly imagine will remain unaffected. But social change cannot so easily be quarantined in this way. Every dinner party or backyard barbecue is abuzz with opinions about what's wrong with Hobart, and confident declarations of what can be done to fix it. Most are based on ideology and wishful thinking. Few proceed from any realistic appraisal of the city's character, its history or its unique circumstances, and few consider what upheavals might be unwittingly set in motion in response.

'People come down here for lifestyle reasons', says the mayor, Rob Valentine:

They get the low stress, the friendliness, the cheaper houses, the great natural environment and quite a good cultural life … But if you look at the socio-economic situation, you find that it's pretty heavily weighted towards the have-nots. There is a certain number of well-off people but I don't know if it's enough to sustain a high-end retail market. There's always the question of how much you want Hobart to be a city of style and glamour as opposed to a city of amenity for a broad population. In the end, commercial activity drives the city, so it's difficult to say that we want this style or that without knowing whether it's going to work.

Long-term resident Dirk Meure, who owns a vine-yard near Kettering, comments:

It's a pleasure to shop in the city and so easy to interact with people, but I don't find Hobart aesthetically pleasing. It's a bit dingy, a bit drab, a bit second-rate. There's no sense of pride in the city. I don't mean the buildings themselves, many of which are beautiful, but the overall presentation. There's a sense of complacency in terms of style, presentation and the theatre of commerce. Yet, at the same time, there's a sort of arrogance: we're the best in the world. It's put about by the branders, the marketeers, the spin doctors, overcompensating for the city's shortcomings.

Nevertheless, as the mayor suggests, the friendliness and ease of shopping might go hand-in-hand with the lack of a sense of theatre. Maybe a slicker, more sophisticated city would be a colder, more aloof one, out of step with people's real needs. As the mayor also points out, it is the market, with its finger on the pulse, that makes the decisions, and the market is pretty strong at the Chickenfeed and Salvo's charity-store end. Spotlight's Harrington Street windows, for example, are an aesthetic disaster, piled with stock and cluttered with disused shelving and remnants. Presumably the shop could smarten itself up if it wanted to, and if it did this whole end of town would benefit, but that might not suit Spotlight's clientele, many of whom find its dagginess reassuring. The city is but a mirror of its inhabitants.

Before embarking on an assignment for a piece about Tasmania, Pauline Webber, a travel writer for

The Australian, was assured by an ex-Tasmanian friend that Hobart's Cat & Fiddle Arcade should not be missed. Only when she found herself standing in this 'functional walkway with its smattering of utilitarian shops' did she realise she'd been conned.[5] Tasmanians (and ex-Tasmanians in particular) have no illusions about their capital city. Yet Webber's friend may have been too cynical. You can find sophistication and style if you know where to look.

You can find it, for example, in some of Salamanca's clubs and bars, or at the very glamorous Henry Jones Art Hotel in Hunter Street, or Norman & Dann's deliciously enticing chocolate shop, or any number of new bars, cafes and coffee shops. Or you could head to the top end of Davey Street, past the grand old sandstone villas. You might not even notice the Islington, but it does not particularly wish to be noticed by people like you. The Islington is ranked by the English magazine *Tatler* as among the one-hundred best in the world, but it has no need to advertise the fact. 'We've now developed a reputation as the benchmark of the small specialist hotel,' says General Manager Amy Parkinson-Bates. 'We've been lucky, though, because we don't really have any competition.'

Everything about it, from the electronic security gate to the antique furniture, the butler (ex-Buckingham Palace) and the art-encrusted library, whispers *exclusivity*. The towels are so big and fluffy you can hardly close your suitcase.

Any hotel of this kind, wherever it is, will present an air of unreality. That, after all, is the point. But here it is particularly apparent. The Islington is a tiny island of privilege and style in a city that struggles to provide a suitable context. 'For the thirty-plus age group with disposable income who like to sit in wine bars and dine elegantly and enjoy the night life, Hobart doesn't have a lot to offer', Amy admits: .

> These people want that big-city choice of lots of different places to go to. There are only two or three really good restaurants in Hobart that we would recommend to our guests for a fine dining experience. On the other hand, since there's little competition, if somebody comes along and does something good it's really going to stand out. If you're in Sydney and you want some trendy Asian fusion restaurant, there's about sixty to choose from. You do one in Hobart and you're going to have the field to yourself. And we've got these great old buildings that you can refurbish in a way that could blow out of the water anything else in Australia.

The Islington's guests include wealthy landowners from the Midlands dropping into town for weddings, anniversaries and birthdays, visitors from Melbourne, Sydney and Brisbane escaping the summer heat and a small number of UK and US tourists.

Despite its glass atrium, marble floors and extensive cellar, the Islington's cosiness and padded comfort – in a word, its *Englishness* – still says 'Tasmania'. 'This sort of venue in Sydney would have to have a much sleeker, more international feel. People in Sydney want to believe they're in New York. But Hobart is Hobart. It has its own special character.'

The folk whose job it is to sell the state to potential tourists like to focus their attention with an exercise they call 'personification'. Some of the images Tourism Tasmania has come up with to personify Hobart are predictable enough: a young woman in an armchair by the fire, a placid water view, Princess Mary and so on. Others are more inventive and revealing. For example, if Hobart were a car, it would be a Toyota Prius – sensible and socially responsible. (By the same reckoning, Sydney might be a Porsche and Melbourne a Range Rover). And the committee's choice of a labrador

as the city's canine personification is inspired, lab-
radors being homely, reliable, eager to please and a
bit slow to catch on. Not glamorous, admittedly,
but amiable. There's a lot to be said for that.

A succession of pasts

Truganini's mother was murdered by sailors, her uncle was shot by a soldier, her sister abducted for sex by sealers, and her fiancé killed by timber workers. Tricked into moving to what was in effect a death camp at Flinders Island in 1835, then to another at Oyster Cove, south of Hobart, she witnessed the slow passing of all those around her, remaining as the sole survivor. Truganini saw out her old age in Hobart, dying there in 1874. Her terrible fears that her body would be desecrated proved well-founded. She was cut up and her skeleton put on display in the Tasmanian Museum, where it remained until 1951.

Henry Jones's mortal remains, on the other hand, were interred at Cornelian Bay Cemetery with great ceremony and respect, attended by some

10000 mourners. His career began in the year Truganini died and by the turn of the century he had become one of Hobart's most powerful businessmen, with fruit-growing, preserving, timber, mining and shipping interests spanning five continents. His jam company was called IXL because, he boasted, 'I excel in whatever I do.'

Truganini and Henry Jones are just two of the Tasmanian identities (almost all of them men) commemorated in bronze on a memorial wall just off Hunter Street, next to the Henry Jones Art Hotel. Others include David Collins, Hobart's first lieutenant governor; Robert Knopwood, its first clergyman and magistrate; composer Peter Sculthorpe; and, inevitably, Errol Flynn.

The inscriptions are crisp and to the point. Their aim is to encourage interest in Tasmania's achievers, perhaps in the hope that we will be moved to emulate them. Henry Jones is lauded for his 'hard work and enterprise', restaurateur George Mure for being 'a fervent advocate of Tasmania and its fisheries and restaurants'. Truganini alone is not accorded any accomplishment. She is present as victim — a remarkable survivor. White people do things, Aboriginal people have things done to them. All the same, the horrors of her story are tactfully passed over. Had you never heard of her before, you might wonder why this woman was being honoured here at all.

Although the memorial wall is a well-intentioned attempt to inspire and inform, it assumes a great deal. When former arts minister Paula Wriedt officially opened it in November 2007 she made all the right noises, but how many in the small gathering that day were left wondering about the actual function of these plaques? What do they tell us? Why are they here? Why these people and not others?

In effect, these soothing inscriptions present what one of Michelle de Kretser's fictional characters, pondering similar memorials in Melbourne, calls '...the willed creation of a sense of the past: a municipal mythmaking ... Cloaked in virtuous intention, these signs functioned insidiously. They displaced history with heritage, plastering over trauma with a picturesque frieze.'[1]

Hunter Street's memorial wall not only ignores the vital distinctions between the material successes of the Henry Joneses on the one hand and, on the other, the enormities of what was done to the Truganinis, reducing both to bland points of interest; it fails to show how the one is connected to the other in a fatal loop of cause and effect.

In short, despite the best will in the world, it is a memorial that flattens out history, stripping it of meaning and purpose.

History is something Tasmanians have always had trouble with. A great deal of it weighs down on them, after all, and it has sometimes been difficult for them to know what to do with it all.

Some commentators have been hard on earlier generations for their wilful forgetting. Peter Hay, for example, has advocated that Van Diemen's Land be restored as the state's name, 'at the expense of the prettifying, shame-derived, "Tasmania"'.[2] Yet poor old Tasmanians in the mid-nineteenth century did have a lot to forget and, however destructive it now seems in hindsight, they can hardly be blamed for wanting to put their ghastly past behind them and start afresh with a new name.

There were three subjects they were anxious to avoid: the shameful way the indigenous inhabitants had been treated, the dreaded 'convict stain', and their own economic woes.

The harrowing story of what happened to the original inhabitants after the British arrived in 1803 is only now being pieced together by historians such as Henry Reynolds and James Boyce. That it was for so long neglected speaks volumes about settler society's unwillingness to acknowledge a large slice of its past. In a postscript to his influential book, *Van Diemen's Land*, Boyce writes:

> With the death of Truganini in 1876, 'full-blood' Aborigines were widely thought to be 'extinct' and their story deemed over. The fact that Truganini's death was contemporaneous with the takeover of the last remaining Aboriginal lands went unnoticed. Colonists could both publicly ponder the tragic consequences of the British conquest and allow its final chapter to proceed almost without comment. Questions about the invasion of Van Diemen's Land were now deemed to be of purely historical interest.[3]

Today, despite Aboriginal political and social issues being so prominent in the news (or perhaps partly as a result), neither the way these people lived before European settlement nor the epic tale of their clash with European culture have succeeded in firing the public's imagination in the way convict history has. Unlike the convicts, indigenous peoples left few traces on the landscape that look interesting from the windows of a passing bus. Tasmania has the world's best collection of Holocene-period mid-dens, for example, but a midden is just a heap of shells to the uninformed. It does not signal any event and it cannot be connected to any individual names, and events and names are what tourists need to latch on to when they seek out connections with the past. While you might admire baskets and shell necklaces, you must go to a museum or gallery to do so, which presupposes a certain level of prior interest and knowledge. It also presupposes a museum. Although that shrine to the convicts, Port Arthur, is Tasmania's most visited tourist attraction and one of its biggest money-earners, there is no major institution devoted to indigenous history and culture. A display at the Tasmanian Museum and Art Gallery, although informative, can hardly do the subject justice. On the face of it, this is astonishing in a city that virtually lives off its history.

When you think about it, however, Port Arthur, less than two hours' drive from Hobart, was already there, with drama and turmoil oozing from every stone. As spectacle its ruins are hard to beat. So making it accessible was easy. Furthermore, the convicts exist solely in the past, safely out of contention, leaving tourists free to imagine them in any way they like. A centre for Aboriginal history and culture, on the other hand, would have to be built from scratch and would be subject to the labyrinthine intricacies of modern indigenous politics.

Sadly, therefore, this large and crucial chunk of Tasmania's history remains fairly much the preserve of ideologues and academic historians. The rest of us must read books and try to imagine. It is enough that civic functions begin with the guests piously 'acknowledging' the Mouheneenner people, serenely confident that no Mouheneenner will appear unexpectedly in the doorway brandishing a spear to spoil their evening.

If Aborigines remain peripheral to the tourist industry's reinvention of the past, convicts occupy centre stage. In one of those dramatic reversals mentioned earlier, Tasmanians have now decided to bring them back from the dead — with a vengeance. Convicts have become almost an obsession.

In the early 1850s, some three-quarters of adult males in Van Diemen's Land were convicts or ex-convicts.[4] In comparison to New South Wales, it was a huge proportion, and it set the mood of Tasmanian society for generations. Long after transportation had ended, and military dictatorship had blossomed into a free democratic state, this continued to be overwhelmingly a prisoner society.

> Because every constructive innovation to improve society was brought up short against the problems persisting from the penal settlement [writes Peter Bolger], it was difficult to avoid morbid obsessions with criminality and moral stain. Behind all of the glorious and satisfying social activities of a free community, the Institute classes, the Royal Society discussions of Aboriginal languages, the pride in new steamships and new gas lighting, there still lay the canker of convict kingdom.[5]

It was not wise to mention convicts in case the person you were talking to had a skeleton in the closet, which was actually quite likely but no less embarrassing for all that. In every second family there lurked a shadowy great-uncle or grandmother who was never to be mentioned. Respectable Hobartians were embarrassed and annoyed that tourists showed so much unhealthy interest in convict history. '[T]he abandoned Port Arthur became, entirely against the wishes of the Tasmanian establishment, the seed from which the island's historical tourism grew.'[6] Even as this was occurring, attempts were being made (in 1889, 1901 and 1913) to demolish Port Arthur's buildings and obliterate the memories they held.

'It's a very strange thing, isn't it,' observes the historian Alison Alexander, 'for everyone just to forget a whole slice of their common history: and for everyone to agree to it.' The 1950s and 1960s, she thinks, were a turning point:

> Tasmania was doing well and Britain had lost
> its influence. People didn't care so much any
> more what the British thought of them. Also,
> the convicts were by this time three or four
> generations back, so it wasn't as if it was your
> grandmother or something. In the seventies,
> there was a huge world-wide interest in family
> histories, and it became easier for people to do
> the research because of microfilm. And, once
> people started doing the research, they found
> that most of the convicts' crimes were minor,
> like stealing handkerchiefs and so on, which
> was not really anything to be ashamed of ...
> People, when they write their family histories,
> will gloss over anything awful their ancestors
> might have done ... So the convicts' story
> could be made into a happy story of larrikins
> and beating the odds ... Their crimes were

completely understandable, they were treated
terribly by the authorities, and when they came
out here they were so brave, so pioneering ...
Remember that this was a time of general anti-
establishment feeling in the community, a time
of rebellion against propriety and respectable
middle-class values.

To continue the thought: the convict story might
also offer a response to those who would reduce
history to a black and white conflict between innocent victims and guilty oppressors. In its inchoate
way, it says, 'Look, our ancestors suffered too. They
were not murderers and invaders but helpless victims'. At a time when competitive victimhood has
become a means of validation, that thought, paradoxically, gives strength.

Whatever the psychological motivations may
have been for this sudden flowering of interest, in
the 1960s and 1970s air travel provided the means
by turning tourism into a major money-earner for
Tasmania, which, apart from its natural beauties,
had little else to sell but its past.

But how to sell it – and to commemorate and
elucidate it – without cheapening, exploiting or vul-
garising the convicts' suffering? It is a problem that

dogs the creators of Holocaust memorials. While you want people to understand what happened to these unfortunate souls and, perhaps, to experience something of what they experienced, you must at the same time try to head off any unseemly fascination. Tales of floggings, solitary confinements, leg-irons and forced labour have a reckless tendency to veer off into ghoulish entertainment: another, even more insidious, form of forgetting that Port Arthur, for all its attributes, has not entirely managed to avoid.

One approach is the poetic one that tries to evoke emotions allusively. The art installations in the Port Arthur Project in 2007, for example, used abstract means to suggest feelings of confinement, loneliness or abandonment. Unfortunately, in their efforts to avoid anything lurid or sensational, the artists drifted instead into languid melancholy, which made the exhibition a strangely limp and bloodless experience, lacking any sense of anger or outrage. Nor were any overt parallels drawn with the injustices of today, suggesting that cruelty and violence are a thing of the past. That distancing is what convict tourism also tends to encourage, whether intentionally or not. It is only the assurance that such horrors could not happen today in civilised countries such as our own that makes our experience of them bearable. The dramas of the past are cordoned off, each carefully composed scene framed by an elaborate proscenium arch and selectively lit. They are rarely allowed to extend far into the world we inhabit today.

Unfortunately, reality has a way of intruding, sometimes catastrophically. In 1996, Port Arthur was unexpectedly revisited by real horror when a disturbed young man named Martin Bryant opened fire randomly, killing thirty-five people and wounding another twenty-one. 'In Tasmania, where so many people, from paramedics to pilots, had been drawn into the vortex created by the shooting,' observed Margaret Scott, 'where everybody knew somebody involved, the disaster became inescapable.'[7] Bryant himself, with a cold logic at once twisted and curiously perceptive, claimed that 'a lot of violence has happened there. It must be the most violent place in Australia. It seemed the right place.'[8]

The legacies of convictism and Aboriginal genocide might have been dealt with more bravely had

Tasmanian society been more robust and self-confident. But that was not the case.

The economic recession that began in 1840 was also experienced by other colonies, but in Tasmania it would drag on for some thirty years. It not only led to the departure of so many young working men and women, as we have seen, but it widened an already corrosive social divide between a small, wealthy (mainly land-owning) elite and the rest of the population. A hundred and fifty years ago, Anthony Trollope attributed Tasmanians' preoccupation with the past – whether obsessing over it or vainly trying to forget it – to their sudden descent into poverty.

> It seems hard to say of a colony, not yet
> seventy years old, that it has seen the best of
> its days, and that it is falling into decay, that
> its short period of importance in the world is
> already gone, and that for the future it must
> exist – as many an old town and old country
> do exist – not exactly on the memory of the
> past, but on the relics which the past left
> behind it.[9]

As it happens, he was wrong about Tasmania being in permanent decline, for eventually it would recover. His prediction that it would have to live off the relics of its past was right, however, but not at all in the way he thought. Instead of being an impoverished society gazing back with regret, as he imagined, Hobart today has begun to prosper by creatively exploiting its earlier ignominy and deprivation. Trollope, who lived at a time when only triumphs and successes were thought worthy of commemoration, would surely have been astonished.

As would those living in Hobart in the 1940s, some seventy years later. As a boy, Vivian Smith felt:

> ... a puzzling sense of loss or absence ... There
> was the history of the Tasmanian aborigines and
> the exterminated tiger; there were decayed and
> abandoned and mouldering and haunted houses;
> factories and buildings that had been condemned;
> there were abandoned ships decaying in the Ships'
> Graveyard at Risdon; cemeteries that were being
> transformed slowly into parks, and cemeteries
> like the one at Queensborough (now completely
> erased) with its crumbling tombs that one could
> wander about in. I am sure I do not exaggerate
> when I say that I grew up in a place that was

> haunted and weighed down by an oppressive past
> and a stagnant present; a world of death and
> decay in a world at war.[10]

Today, visitors clamber out of buses at the entrance
to the Female Factory in South Hobart full of
expectation. Female factories, or workhouses, were
a uniquely Australian response to the management
of convict women, and this, they have been assured,
is the only remaining example. As soon as they walk
in through the gap in the huge stone wall, however, they are brought up short. There is practically
nothing there. Just a big, empty courtyard. They
wander around aimlessly for a while, poking into
nooks and crannies in the hope of finding something – anything – to excite their interest, then file
back onto the bus bewildered.

They have been brought face-to-face with that
'puzzling sense of loss or absence' that troubled
the young Vivian Smith. But whereas for him it
represented death and decay, for today's tourists
it is simply a blank to which no emotion can be
attached. What they are being asked to do at the
Female Factory, as at so many other historical sites,
is to use their imaginations to supply what is missing, with the help of commentary provided by the

guides ('This is where the cells used to be'). This demands personal resources they may not possess.

Tourists on the Hobart Explorer Tram, trundling along Macquarie Street (it is not really a tram but a bus dressed up as one), gaze mutely out at service stations, bottle shops and office buildings while the cheery voice of Ken, their driver, briskly tries to fill the blanks. He knows when every old building was built and he can regale them with colourful tales of Hobart's 'characters'. He can show them where the real trams used to run and where weirs were constructed across the rivulet. They dutifully raise their digital cameras in ritual obeisance at every point of interest. Yet, if they finish their tour feeling somewhat unfulfilled, it is because facts are not really what they had come in search of. They are not particularly fussed about whether that warehouse is Georgian or late Victorian, or that this house was designed by John Lee Archer, or that it was once a brothel or the site of a murder. They don't know whether his facts are accurate and will almost certainly not bother to find out, because, frankly, they don't know what to do with the information.

They have come to Hobart to time-travel: the same reason they might go to Venice, Prague or

Persepolis (and the same reason they watch BBC costume dramas on television). In Australia, this is usually possible only in museums and designated historical sites, which serve a subtly different, more didactic, purpose. It is difficult, in this country, for people to escape the present, which is everywhere around them, intruding and dominating, reducing the historical to a sideshow in thrall to modern economic demands. They want to experience a different world, to know that other lives are possible, to fill in the blanks. They want to know what it *felt* like to be alive in another epoch. Ballarat gives it to them in spades, as do Ross and Oatlands in the Tasmanian Midlands. Hobart, at least those parts of it where disruption to the historical fabric has been minimal, comes a pretty good second, but only to those who get out of the tourist buses to experience more than just scenery. In Battery Point and Salamanca, the present can be enjoyed as if it were a part of history, rather than the other way around.

This is not empty nostalgia. As John Berger writes in *Pig Earth,* 'the past is never behind. It is always to the side.' Adam Nicolson, expanding on the idea, suggests that: 'Nothing is intelligible without the past, not because it is the past, but because it is the missing body of the present.'[11] Our immersion in historical places provides a way of seeing life from a different perspective, with new eyes, informed by different criteria. It is a way of bracketing off our mundane everyday existences in order to understand them more clearly and, perhaps, to live them more meaningfully.

This is something the lace-and-bonnets style of historical tourism rarely comes to grips with. In Alison Alexander's opinion:

> Historical tourism has got into the hands of the folkloric people who don't know any history. It's soppy, sentimental stuff. Stories are okay, but they should be accurate stories. If the stories are accurate and well told and the people telling them are interesting and sympathetic and don't sound as though they're telling them for the hundredth time, then it's fine ... but I don't think that in Tasmania enough effort has been put into it, or enough scholarship.

Heritage tourism is, admittedly, far more sophisticated and subtle in its approaches now than it once was. It is no longer just about herding people into buses and feeding them information: it offers personally escorted walks, specialised tours and historical re-enactments (for example, the inventive Louisa's Walk, in which actors re-create one convict woman's story in the places where it occurred), along with more creative opportunities for visitors to determine their own pace and follow their own instincts.

Yet all these initiatives – whether they be private commercial concerns or the pet projects of enthusiastic volunteers – are forced into the position of glossing what happens to remain, most of it (the Female Factory being the most obvious example) critically underdeveloped. Successive state governments have been more than happy to leave the work to others.

How terribly odd to expend so much energy attracting people to the state while paying so little attention to providing them with things to do once they get here.

So much for visitors, but what about those who live here? While Venice, Paris and Ballarat present invigorating stories of enterprise, wealth and success, Hobart's are grim ones of struggle against the odds. What effect does it have on a society to dwell on such a past? How does all that violence, poverty and despair impinge upon the present?

Well, one answer is that it doesn't, at least not in any morbid way. Anyone who has moved to Hobart in the past ten or fifteen years will have trouble understanding the 'whisper of death' that Gwen Harwood detected. The successful commodification of history has objectified it and turned it into a game, displacing 'history with heritage, plastering over trauma with a picturesque frieze', as Michelle de Kretser put it. No longer is there any need to shove the horrors of the past under the rug to fester in the darkness. Nothing is off-limits now because no shame, iniquity or past embarrassment has moral force any more. Even the blood-and-guts tale of Alexander Pearce's cannibalism makes for good Sunday-night television.

Twenty years ago, Peter Conrad wrote: 'New countries aren't supposed to have a history. But if anything, Tasmania possesses too much history: a succession of pasts, queuing up like unappeased revenants to accuse the ignorant present.'[12]

He could almost get away with that sort of thing then, but even he might have second thoughts today, when Tasmania's pasts are queuing up, not like unappeased revenants, but unending banquets laid out to satisfy the rapaciously curious present.

The remarkable flowering of interest in Tasmania's history over the past twenty years or so may be seen as atonement, or even perhaps overcompensation, for earlier neglect. People may still feel they want to escape the past, or they may be in love with it (two sides of the same coin really), but they no longer feel intimidated by it.

At the State Library in Murray Street you will find books on almost every conceivable aspect of Tasmanian history. There are specialised studies on the rivulet and the mountain and histories of food and wine, art and education, the whaling industry, trams and hydro-electricity; there is a plethora of historical novels and personal memoirs; there are countless volumes of old photographs; there are modern reprints of books by Anthony Trollope, Louisa Anne Meredith and Marcus Clark; there are histories of Clarence, Sandy Bay, Battery Point, Glenorchy and the Eastern Shore; there is a guide to Tassie Terms and a weighty *Companion to Tasmanian History*. And, of course, there are innumerable accounts of aspects of convict and Aboriginal histories, from the populist to the highly specialised. Go through to the Tasmaniana Library and the quantity (and quality) of published material there is astonishing, given Tasmania's size and population. In the reading room, students, pensioners, young mothers and office workers on lunchbreaks lean earnestly into microfilm viewers to scan old newspapers; or they jostle for space in the archives office in the hope of finding convicts or Aborigines among their ancestors; or they research the histories of their localities, their streets or the houses they live in; or look for evidence to win an argument; or simply indulge their personal passions.

Tasmanian history is also the mainstay of bookshops, and local history groups are attracting more interest than ever before. 'I do think Tasmanians are more interested and involved in their history than people in other states,' says Alison Alexander, 'probably because this is a small community. The history is self-contained and manageable.' It is also more personal: the historical figure you discover might turn out to have been your great-grandfather's second cousin, or you might discover that someone famous once occupied the house you live in. Even if you don't, the stories you uncover are bound to connect.

If anything, Hobartians are becoming satiated by their banquets of history. Perhaps, strictly speaking, Conrad was right about there being too much of it, although not about its effects, which are anything but baleful. The danger of all this concentration on the past lies not so much in making us gloomy or pessimistic, but rather in its potential to make our present lives seem rather eventless and inauthentic by comparison – merely the froth floating on top of a solid mass of yesterdays. In no other Australian city does the past impinge upon the present so frequently or so insistently.

Inevitably, fault lines occur where the manufactured romance of the past meets the necessities of the present. They are nicely encapsulated in Harrington Street, between Collins and Liverpool, where the sturdy sandstone parapet of a bridge over the Hobart Rivulet bears an odd inscription, carefully carved in elegant Roman lettering: 'ERECTED AD 1844 / RE-ERECTED AD 1968'. When the original stone bridge was found to be too low to cope with the occasional flood and was replaced by a functional concrete span, someone had the bright idea of re-assembling one of its walls. The updated inscription is both an honest admission that this is not the original structure and a form of reparation for its destruction: a nice touch, except that a public lavatory has been built behind the parapet and garlanded with coils of barbed wire. This theatrical little assemblage is a small masterpiece of absurdity: a handsome, historicized remnant of convict days grandly setting the scene for a grubby little breezeblock dunny. It speaks volumes about Hobart's conflicted attitudes to its many pasts.

Nature within cooee

Hobart never completely surrounds you in a hard carapace of urbanisation. Even at its heart, you are no more than a cooee from mountain, forest or water. Fingers of bushland follow the creeks and rivulets down the slopes into the suburbs, where the city council maintains more than 190 kilometres of walking tracks and bush trails.

Nature is not only close at hand, but richly varied. The half-hour drive from river to mountaintop takes you from coastal scrub through dry open woodland, tall dense forest, sub-alpine woodland and finally alpine moorland above the snowline, where tough, leathery little bushes cling to life in crevices between the rocks.

When they get there, most visitors gaze down upon the city spread out map-like far below them, searching out familiar streets or buildings to establish their bearings. The few who turn in the other direction, towards the west, are faced with a far more awesome prospect, across vast expanses of forest towards the ocean. The nearest human habitation is 11 000 kilometres away in Patagonia.

The mountain and the bush that clothes it mean different things to different people. To the early settlers, stranded on a tiny island of civilisation within a wild, unknown island of wilderness, it could only have been threatening and overwhelming. The bush seemed especially dangerous because it was very rugged and pressed so close, and because the weather was notoriously unpredictable. A family picnic in the foothills was all very well, but things could turn sour at a moment's notice. Truth and superstition intertwined in tales about the terrible fate that awaited any careless youngster who wandered off. Amidst those dank, gloomy forests, Aboriginal giants and ferocious creatures lurked, ready to pounce. As colonial infants lay awake at night listening to the distant shrieks of Tasmanian devils, fully aware that others just like themselves had disappeared without trace, their imaginations raced with fascination and fear.

While delighted by 'the many rare and beautiful plants inhabiting its wild and almost inaccessible glens and ravines', Louisa Anne Meredith, in the mid-nineteenth century, could not resist the Romantic allure of Mount Wellington's sinister side. 'Several unfortunate persons who at various times have imprudently attempted the ascent without a guide, have never returned, nor has any vestige of them ever been discovered'.[1] This was true enough, but the legends that accumulated around such disappearances tapped into something darker and more tangled.

That something owed as much to race-memory as it did to observed reality. It was part of the European – or more specifically English – Romantic legacy. When the botanist Robert Brown, during five months at the Hobart settlement in 1804, traipsed up, down and around Mount Wellington and all through the wet rainforests of the Huon Valley, he was ostensibly seeking scientific knowledge, in the great tradition of Enlightenment thinkers. But the sheer determination with which he pursued his endeavours, and the extraordinary privations he chose to put himself through, suggest something of the thrill he felt at pitting himself against nature. As Brown would well have understood, the sublime lay not just in what was seen or experienced. Its emotional impact depended on recollections, myths, and cultural experiences filtered through art, music and poetry.

Paradoxically, the knowledge gained by Brown and the scientists, explorers and naturalists who followed him would gradually demythologise the Australian bush, banishing the wood-sprites and monsters and rendering it friendly, sunny and full of wonder. Yet, in poetic imaginings, the malady lingered on, and lingers to this day. The Tasmanian Museum and Art Gallery is full of colonial – and even some contemporary – works of art that strive to make the mountain menacing and unknowable again: bathed in ethereal light, burdened by unnaturally dark clouds, or larger than life so that it bears down like a malevolent force on the defenceless little city below.

Peter Conrad recalls that his childhood:

> …was overshadowed by a brutal, bad-tempered
> eminence: a mountain … it looms suddenly
> above the city and grimaces from a height of four
> thousand feet; it squeezes the settlement, denying
> it toehold … It terminates every view, and
> invigilates every backyard.'[2]

Environmentalist Bob Brown takes the thought and

gives it a twist of reverence: 'The mountain shapes the character of the city,' he says, 'and therefore it shapes the character of us. This mountain sets the mood of our city, which is different from every other city in Australia.'[3]

We have all felt it, of course: that shudder of dread, that feeling of insignificance in the face of nature's vast inscrutability. It is what we go on bushwalks to experience. It is why we stand on rocky pinnacles or plunge into rainforests. And we don't have to go far. It is necessary only to get out of the car and venture a hundred metres or so off the main road at suburban Fern Tree, pausing in the cold, misty air amongst the serpent-like fronds of tree ferns, with eucalypt trunks soaring overhead, to sense something of that shudder of dread that so disturbed earlier generations.

Its residues may be found in the racks of wilderness postcards, calendars and souvenir books in any Hobart newsagency or bookshop. The terrain they depict – wild, isolated and lofty – is exactly the kind that one might get lost in, never to be found again. Except, of course, that today roads, walking tracks, helicopters and satellite navigation have considerably lessened the odds.

There are other, more constructive and less

culturally loaded ways to appreciate the bush. Generations of Hobart children have derived innocent delight in the surrounding countryside without concern for its moral import. As a boy, Henry Reynolds lived in West Hobart, with wooded Mount Knocklofty at his doorstep:

> The bush was indeed our domain. From quite an
> early age my friends and I would 'go up the bush'
> and sometimes be away all day. As we got older
> our expeditions became more elaborate and we
> pushed further up into the foothills of Mount
> Wellington. Our parents weren't negligent; it
> just seemed to be accepted that we could roam
> where we wished – almost for as long as we liked,
> particularly if we had taken lunch with us.[4]

Author Tim Bowden, as a child in Sandy Bay in the 1950s, spent many happy hours exploring the nearby forests on Mount Nelson.

As Elizabeth Christensen and MC Jones recall in their delightful memoir of growing up on the Eastern Shore:

> Lindisfarne was a perfect place for children, who
> could safely be left to roam where they pleased.
> They built billy-carts and in the holidays loaded
> them with rabbit traps and frying pans and tents

and spent almost all day rambling round to Shones Corner or Risdon, stopping for a spot of birdnesting at the old limekilns on the way. There were some lovely spots among the willows along the creek where they set up a little camp and sometimes stayed for a couple of nights.[5]

Aside from the occasional snake and the risk of a fall, the bush was a safe enough playground.

From such untroubled identification a new myth has arisen. Today's Tasmania promotes itself as clean, green and pristine, an untouched natural paradise, inviting you to 'lose yourself on an eco-adventure' without any chance of frightening you off. The sublime has given way to childlike wonder. Yet the underlying motivations are little changed: Tasmanians remain a particularly mythopoeic people.

The test of a good myth is the extent to which various groups with differing outlooks are able to co-opt it to their own ends. For environmentalists, 'clean green' Tasmania represents an ideal of purity and innocence; for politicians, a campaigning tool; for tourism, a brand; for food growers, a niche market; for the woodchipping industry, camouflage; for Tasmanians unaligned with any of the above, it is what sets them apart and makes them feel good about themselves.

Few would have dreamt of embracing the 'clean and green' myth, nor found it at all useful, had it not been for a particular turning point in the 1970s, one that may rank as Hobart's most significant contribution to the modern world. Historians Martin Mulligan and Stuart Hill have pointed out that:

> Although Tasmanians cannot, of course, claim the green movement as their own, they are central to its unfolding as a political force. For much of the [conservation] movement, the focus continued to be on the preservation of 'pristine' wilderness and the pinnacle of this preservationist movement probably came with the campaign to prevent the flooding of the Franklin River in the south-west corner of Tasmania in the late 1970s and early 1980s. While the Franklin campaign can be seen as a continuation of the preservationist movement of old, it also represents a turning point in the way that wilderness issues were taken directly into the political arena and it led to the birth of a green political party, firstly in Tasmania and then nationally.[6]

The Franklin is not near Hobart, of course, but the campaign to save it, like the anti-transportation push that eventually brought an end to convictism in 1853, was initiated and managed largely by city dwellers. It was only after Bob Brown had given up his medical practice in Launceston and moved to Hobart in 1979 to devote himself to the Franklin campaign that it really began to gain traction. He had to be near the politicians who were making the decisions. It is fair to say that it was urban dwellers who, from the start, led the way in the politicisation of nature preservation. This is not to denigrate the efforts of some farmers and country-town dwellers, but simply to acknowledge that only in the city did people have opportunities to form groups, publish, communicate effectively with one another and negotiate directly with those in power. Unionists and politicians who sneer at 'urban greenies' fail to understand (or choose to ignore) this simple fact.

While it was undoubtedly a turning point, the Franklin campaign did not by any means mark the beginning of environmental advocacy. In the nineteenth century, many colonists developed great affection for particular areas of bush around the city. 'Scenery preservation', as it was rather quaintly called, was an important priority, at least for an influential minority. Artists and writers helped to promote an appreciation for nature that cut across class divisions, influencing not only the aesthetically aware, but ordinary recreational sailors (even today, you don't have to be rich to have a boat in Hobart), fishers, bushwalkers and families who escaped to their mountain or seaside shacks at weekends. 'There is a trilling and graceful play in the landscape of this country', the English artist John Glover had enthused after his arrival in Van Diemen's Land in 1831,[7] and gradually, as their leisure time increased, the locals came to share that view.

Their awareness brought increasing alarm at what was being done to their beloved bushland. They began to assert themselves. A campaign in the 1930s against the construction of a road to Mount Wellington's summit was so keenly fought that many people look back on it today as the first stirring of the local environmental movement. Suburban councils, to their credit, responded with legislation to stop the destruction of trees and parklands and to establish green belts, although they had to be persuaded. In the mid-1950s, a spirited campaign to 'Save the Bays' (specifically New Town Bay) from industrial encroachments mobilised the people of Glenorchy. Like most such campaigns, it succeeded and failed in about equal measure.

Then, in 1972, a bitterly fought, and ultimately unsuccessful, campaign to save Lake Pedder in south-western Tasmania from a Hydro-Electric Commission dam gave the fledgling environmental movement its big cause. The flooding of this serene body of water and hundreds of square kilometres of surrounding wilderness brought Tasmania to the attention of the entire nation, although not in a way that anyone would have wanted. It gave rise to the United Tasmania Group – the world's first green political party – and the Tasmanian Wilderness Society, both of which would grow into organisations of national importance.

So the fledgling Greens sprouted from well-established roots. They were fertilized by Tasmania's Hare-Clark proportional representation voting system, which tends to advantage minor parties, and, obliquely, by the intransigence of the state Labor Party, which, at the behest of the Construction, Forestry, Mining and Energy Union, has never made any secret of its hostility to environmental concerns.

Although the conservation movement is usually pictured as being politically radical – that is certainly the way its enemies wish to see it – in fact it is an odd and slightly uncomfortable mix of the revolutionary and reactionary. The religiosity behind campaigns to save 'pristine wilderness' originates in the nineteenth-century American transcendentalists' pre-Darwinian worship in Nature's Cathedral, and the ideal of the simple life in tune with Mother Nature looks back longingly to the anti-modernism of the Amish and the Shakers.

It is not entirely insignificant, then, that green politics arose and flourished in a city that not only had more nature than others, but also a strong tradition of social conservatism, nostalgia and religious observance. Dennis Altman, returning to the state of his birth in 1983 after a long absence, noticed the growth of a counter-culture:

> ...with young refugees from the mainland moving into cheap land and housing in the Huon Valley, which stretches along the coast south of Hobart. Counter-cultural, perhaps [he adds ruefully], but a conservative version, largely made up of young families, in which the men tilled the fields while the women stayed at home with the children. A number are committed Christians, living lives rather like those of the Huon Valley sixty years earlier.[8]

Not surprisingly, given the battles over woodchipping that have soured Tasmanian politics for decades, Hobart people love their trees. For many, nature conservation simply means tree preservation and more than a few symbolic battles have been fought over local specimens to which residents have formed sentimental attachments. There is little use in pointing out that the one they have chained themselves to is diseased or about to fall on the neighbour's roof. To fight for the retention of a tree is to strike a blow for moral values over expediency. Gestures have their own intrinsic moral weight.

Eucalypts are the most prized, especially those grand, gnarled, solitary ones that journalists like to call 'majestic'. Oaks, elms and pines — emblems of Hobart's supposed Englishness — are also defended by those who, quite rightly, consider them as much a part of the city's heritage as its Georgian buildings.

In 1919, Governor and Lady Newdegate planted two saplings at a Soldiers Memorial Avenue on the Domain. These were trees of high symbolic value: His Lordship's an oak brought as an acorn from Gallipoli by a young man with 'Tasmanian blood in his veins'; Her Ladyship's a laurel, said to be from the Forum in Rome. In his tribute to the fallen at the solemn ceremony, Lord Newdegate intoned:

> It is easy to put up monuments of stone to their memory, and we are glad to do so, but I think the idea of planting trees, which, as the years go on, will grow and increase, is splendid, because when people come and walk along your beautiful domain they will see those trees growing, and will always be reminded that they were planted in memory of those who, without fear, had gone and done what they considered their duty [an interesting turn of phrase, this]. I am sure it will be a labour of love with the people of Hobart to see that the trees are properly looked after.[9]

And so it was – for a while. Then memories began to fade, the commemoration of wars lost its social cachet, and the Soldiers' Memorial Avenue (or Soldiers Walk as it was now called) fell on hard times. A rubbish tip, a sports field and a car park encroached on its hallowed grounds. More recently, however, as the Howard government revved up the Gallipoli fiasco as a focus of national pride, the Friends of Soldiers Walk was formed to restore it, which involved the felling of some Tasmanian blue gums in favour of more symbolically appropriate European species.

If oak, elm and ash evoked Britain and the Empire, wattles, gums and banksias (although nowhere near as nice) embodied the spirit of the future: proud, independent and optimistic. The indomitable Lady Franklin made the allegory manifest in the 1830s with a 'Collection of our indigenous Plants' at Sassafras Valley on the New Town Rivulet. She gathered them around a mock-Greek temple she called Ancanthe, in case anyone should doubt that, wherever the colony's growing tips might be headed, its roots remained firmly in fertile Enlightenment soil. The renowned botanist Joseph Hooker, friend and confidante of Charles Darwin, visited Ancanthe several times, declaring himself most impressed.[10] It fell into disrepair after the Franklins departed, taking their lofty ideals with them, but it, too, is now restored.

From the earliest years of settlement, Hobart gardens included native plants alongside the geraniums, wallflowers and stocks, although more for practical than sentimental reasons. Tea-tree, heart berry, bauera, snow daisy, olearia, mountain pepper and many other small, garden-friendly bushes could be collected from nearby mountain slopes. They bore a passing resemblance to the more familiar imported shrubs but, unlike them, cost nothing. Yet, over time, they became a commercial proposition. In 1884, F Lipscombe, Nursery Seedsman of Sandy Bay, could proudly call himself a 'grower and collector of indigenous seeds and plants', confident that he could make a living.[11]

Today, here as elsewhere, natives are all the rage. A specialist nursery at Ridgeway, halfway up the mountain, stocks nothing but Tasmanian plants, a surprisingly large proportion of which are found nowhere else in the world, such as the deciduous beech (*Nothofagus gunnii*: the only native whose leaves change colour and fall completely in autumn), and the extraordinary, prehistoric *richea*. Even those with a firm grasp of the native flora of the mainland can find it all bewilderingly unfamiliar.

The symbolic language of plants has subtleties that are easily misinterpreted. For example, Governor Sir James Plimsoll's Australian native garden at Government House, installed in 1987, is generally acknowledged to have been a noble idea misplaced. The straggly, open habit of tea-trees and banksias looks quite out of place against primly manicured expanses of lawn. Nothing else at Government House is permitted to straggle. The natives are a victory of well-intentioned ideology over sensitivity. On the front lawn, however, a couple of mature blue gums that frame the view from the reception room down the Derwent Estuary are acceptable because, in their proud isolation, they function as honorary Europeans. One was planted by the Queen, its less vigorous companion by the Duke of Edinburgh. It is a curious fact that trees ceremonially installed at Government House by notable women invariably outgrow those planted by their husbands.

Around 1831, John Glover walked from his home in Melville Street to nearby Mount Knocklofty, where he set up his easel at a picturesque spot known locally as Salvator Rosa Glen. (Those with some knowledge of art history will see the significance of the name.) The resultant painting – *The River Derwent and Hobart Town* – which now hangs in the Tasmanian Museum and Art Gallery, looks down on the little settlement from a considerable height, framing it with foreground hills. South Arm can be seen in the far distance.

If you go to this glen today – it is a popular walking and picnic area – you will find Glover's work reproduced on a panel at the exact spot it was painted. What will immediately strike you is that the bare, rocky slopes he observed are now entirely sheathed in growth, to the extent that his view of Hobart has been almost entirely obscured. This remarkable transformation has been wrought by the Friends of Knocklofty, one of several volunteer bushcare groups that flourish in Kangaroo Valley, Wellington Park, Fern Tree, South Hobart, Sandy Bay and elsewhere. They gather at weekends in overalls and sensible shoes to clear gorse, broom and Spanish heath and restore creeks, parks and reserves, leaving behind forests of plastic guards that, with luck and good management, will blossom into urban greenery. In selflessly toiling for the good of all, they rekindle that sense of belonging and sharing so important to the many small, close-knit communities of which Hobart is composed. These friends foster neighbourliness.

Astrid Wright, the convenor of the Knocklofty group, is, like many of her companions, a veteran environmental campaigner.

> I was involved in the Franklin campaign and active for many years in the Wilderness Society, and I've been a keen bushwalker since I arrived in Tasmania in 1974. Now that I'm older and more settled, I'm less able to be active in bigger environmental issues

so I take more interest in my local area. For me,
now, this is a more manageable way of caring.

> It would be nice to have some younger ones, but I
> think it's better that they are out trying to protect
> the Styx and the Florentine, looking after the
> bigger picture. I hope they will come to their local
> bushcare groups when they are older, as I did.

She is not especially concerned that almost all the
group's members are over fifty:

> It would be nice to have some younger ones, but I
> think it's better that they are out trying to protect
> the Styx and the Florentine, looking after the
> bigger picture. I hope they will come to their local
> bushcare groups when they are older, as I did.

Astrid is full of praise for the Hobart City Council, which, she says, provides a wealth of practical
assistance and manages the group's funding. 'They
are fully involved and very co-operative: much more
interested in bushcare than most councils.'

Sometimes, though, trees are planted where not
everyone agrees they should be. The grassy area
at the foot of Knocklofty where Henry Reynolds
played as a boy was once a popular spot for picnics, recreation and courting couples. Today it is,
like Salvator Rosa Glen, thickly wooded. Yet, as
Reynolds points out, it was cleared for farming in
the early nineteenth century and, being near a permanent spring, may also have been kept treeless by
Aborigines. 'I can't help thinking,' he writes,

...that the fate of my overgrown common reflects wider truths about Tasmania, which is cherished and celebrated as a place rather than as a society with history and heritage. There is still a lack of awareness about Aboriginal land use and the way in which they managed, shaped and humanised the landscape.[12]

If you look carefully at *The River Derwent and Hobart Town*, you will notice, to the right, a tall eucalypt that has recently been burnt by fire. Remarkably, Glover accurately depicts the new growth sprouting all along its trunk, something that would have been completely foreign to him. Presumably, the tree was the victim of wildfire, although the seasonal burning of the bush by Aborigines had continued around the town's outskirts until at least 1818.

The risk of fire is, of course, the downside to having forests on the doorstep. Although not normally prone to the searing summer heat of Melbourne and Adelaide, Hobart's dryness and windiness make it particularly vulnerable to fires. Almost from the beginning, they terrified the settlers, who understood little about the conditions that caused them or how to deal with them.

A major outbreak swept into the outer suburbs in 1854, leading to legislation permitting the declaration of what we would now call fire-ban days. By far the worst blaze, however, occurred in 1967. It swept on two fronts through Upper Sandy Bay, West Hobart, Dynnyrne, South Hobart and Lenah Valley, almost completely surrounding the city, where people fled in panic, blinded by smoke and ash. Sixty-two were killed and 420 city buildings destroyed. It was, says the author Roger McNeice, 'a disaster of enormous magnitude in southern Tasmania, the blackest day in the history of the state.'[13]

'The devastation is heart-breaking,' Gwen Harwood wrote to an interstate friend:

> I always thought of the lovely Lenah Valley track
> as *permanent*, but it's gone. There are great deposits
> of powdery earth and ashes that will wash into
> the creek at the first rain. We didn't see a living
> creature except for the lizards, ants, and a few
> wrens. The mountain parrots have gone, the brush
> wattle birds, the flame-breasted robins, the pink
> robins, even the clinking currawongs. They say
> that hawks and crows were washed up in hundreds
> along the shores of the Derwent, unharmed by
> flame but asphyxiated by the smoke. Some of
> the great myrtle gullies have been burnt out – we
> really don't know if anything survived on our side
> of the mountain. Do you remember the Springs

Hotel [halfway up the mountain]? Among its
ruins we found a lovely cup of Bavarian china
which we set out as an offering to the gods.[14]

The Springs Hotel, which had always been a financial liability, was never rebuilt, although proposals
surface from time to time then quietly slip away
again. Its remains can still be seen amongst the
undergrowth.

Yet there were those who saw opportunity even
in this heartbreak. As Tim Bowden recalls:

A rabidly pro-north friend, Robin Wyly, once told
me that shortly after the 1967 bushfires which
ravaged the south, he saw a hand-lettered sign in
a Launceston shop window saying: WANTED: 167
GOOD MEN AND TRUE TO MARCH ON THE SOUTH
WHILE THEY'RE STILL WEAK.[15]

What the forestry industry, with Orwellian guile,
calls 'regeneration burns' – huge conflagrations
sparked by napalm dropped from aircraft onto the
residues of bulldozed forests – present little direct
threat to city properties. However, if the wind is
blowing from the wrong direction, vast palls of
smoke from autumn burns in the Huon Valley can
choke the city for days, reducing the sun to an eerie
orange ball and confining indoors those with respi-

ratory problems. In 2008, the burn-offs coincided with Easter holidays, leaving tourists gasping for air and tourism operators fuming. As one visitor complained:

> …it was oppressive and quite ugly: the lowering sun shining through the smoke turned the river black with dull red highlights and the golden grass to rust colours, and almost the whole sky was a murky grey-brown. The smoke was coming down to ground level too, and we could smell it in the air. We might have stayed in the Huon Valley for the evening, looking around the craft shops and galleries and maybe buying something before finding somewhere nice for dinner but did not want to stay under that choking pall any longer than we had to.[16]

The state government and Forestry Tasmania rushed into damage control, guaranteeing that nothing of the sort would happen again. 'We don't want a repeat of last autumn', said Forestry Tasmania's head of fire management, Tony Blanks.[17] No, indeed we don't. That does not mean reducing the number of burns, however, of which some 400 were being planned by Mr Blanks at the time. It means organising their timing to make them less apparent, ensuring that Tasmania's clean, green image remains unblemished. Perceptions must be changed, not realities.

Crossing the Derwent in a dinghy could be life-threatening in the early days of settlement because whales had an unnerving habit of surfacing unexpectedly beneath boats. So numerous were they that their calls kept Hobart folk awake at night. Black swans were also common, and made an easy, nourishing meal. They survived, and can be seen in great numbers today in shallow waters beside the highway at Bridgewater. Much to the delight of the locals, even the whales, after a long absence, are starting to return.

Eating mussels or oysters from the heavily polluted river is certainly not recommended, but those who catch leatherjacket, flathead and trout from boats or headlands in the estuary appear to be healthy enough, whatever chemical cocktails might be accumulating in their bloodstreams. Ralphs Bay, Cornelian Bay, Otago Bay and other sheltered spots provide havens for wading birds, although development is slowly driving them away.

As the Derwent is gradually cleaned up, through the combined efforts of the state government and local industries, fur seals and dolphins appear near the city centre increasingly often, although they are still novel enough to cause a flurry of attention and maybe a photograph in the newspaper. A seal, unimaginatively nicknamed Sammy, turns up from time to time around the fish punts at Sullivans Cove, just over the road from Parliament House, showing off and cadging meals. He seems to enjoy being a tourist attraction, confident that, as one of a protected species, he is safe from harm.

All over the suburbs, ringtail and brushtail possums steal fruit and clatter across roofs, frogs croak hypnotically in backyard ponds, skinks warm themselves on footpaths, and wattle birds cry 'ellicot, ellicot' from the banksias. If you live a bit further out, you might be rewarded with a bettong or Tasmanian pademelon outside your back door (both are extinct on the mainland) or be forced to suffer bandicoots digging up your lawn.

Given this wealth of active wildlife, it may seem odd that the one given the most attention is long gone. Perhaps this is only to be expected, in fact, since humans have a habit of mythologising what they have successfully eliminated: the more threatened a species is, the more admired; the more successful in adapting to human encroachment, the more disdained. Today, the Tasmanian tiger (thylacine), hounded to extinction some seventy years ago, is everywhere you look: on the state government's logo, tourist brochures, websites and countless commercial products from tee-shirts, beer mugs and calendars to campervans. It even peers out from car numberplates, with the slogan 'Tasmania: explore the possibilities', suggesting, perhaps, that extinction is one of the possibilities we are being invited to explore. One of the saddest sights Hobart has to offer is a few minutes of grainy black-and-white film screening continuously at the Tasmanian Museum and Art Gallery, showing Benjamin, the last known tiger, forlornly pacing his concrete pen at Beaumaris Zoo, just before he died in 1936.

The Hobart City Council coat of arms features another extinct creature – the Tasmanian emu – along with the Forester kangaroo which, in this state, only narrowly escaped the same fate. Tasmania is full of absences.

Hobartians are great keepers of pets: nature brought to heel. They are blessed with plenty of backyard space and, since many grew up on farms, they have become accustomed to sharing their lives with animals. Barking dogs, meowing cats and contentedly clucking chooks are as much a part of the suburban soundtrack as squealing tyres and hissing cappuccino machines. A far greater proportion of households have dogs than in any other Australian capital city. It seems only appropriate, then, that the first dog show ever held in Australia opened in 1862 at 'Mr Moore's Horse Bazaar in Hobart Town', with 'prizes ... awarded to the owners of the best bred Dogs of both sexes.' Among the entries was an impeccably bred labrador belonging to the state governor, Colonel Thomas Gore-Brown.[18]

Touchingly, several local councils today set aside beaches for canine recreation, the most popular being a huge stretch of foreshore at Kingston where, in daily scenes of unalloyed joy, German shepherds, poodles, spaniels and foxies splash together in the waves, fetching sticks, retrieving balls and good-naturedly sniffing bums. It provides the perfect antidote to world-weariness. A small minority who appear to prefer world-weariness lodge complaints from time to time but are met with well-organised resistance. The Hobart council was recently forced into retreat with its tail between its legs when public rallies scuttled its plan to restrict dog-walking at Cornelian Bay. In a small city, networks are easily maintained, allowing lobby groups to mobilise quickly.

Eight years before Hobart's dogs strutted their stuff at Mr Moore's, Hobart also hosted Australia's first poultry exhibition, organised by the Ornithological Society of Tasmania, now the Southern Tasmanian Poultry Club. Locally bred birds included black swans, but fancy imported breeds naturally attracted all the attention. The club's shows still attract big crowds today, and are duly reported in the local paper. There is nothing glamorous or self-consciously promotional about them: they are, as one visitor was heard to remark as she held her nose against the smell, 'really authentic'. The great popularity of such displays reminds us once again of the city's living agrarian connections.

'Cool off in Tasmania'

Charles Darwin, who climbed laboriously to the top of Mount Wellington in February 1836, was unimpressed, declaring it to be 'of little picturesque beauty ...' In contrast, the novelist Jessie Couvreur gushed: 'Tiers of hills rose one above the other in grand confusion, until they culminated in the towering height of Mount Wellington, keeping guard in majestic silence over the lonely little city that encircled its base.'[1] (Mount Wellington is the culmination of a long mountain range, so it would not, in fact, be possible for Hobart to encircle its base. It is the mountains that encircle Hobart.) Not for the last time would scientific and artistic opinions diverge, with both, to our perceptions, getting it slightly wrong. Trollope, with his unerring eye for social manners, mischievously declared it to be 'just enough of a mountain to give excitement to ladies and gentlemen in Middle life', whatever that might actually mean.[2]

Regardless of whether you think of the mountain as majestic, brooding, malevolent or inspiring, what everyone agrees on is its usefulness as a weather guide. Its peak, perfectly clear one minute, can be obscured in an eye-blink by descending fingers of downy white cloud bearing thin veils of misty rain, which, just as quickly, will be driven off by shafts of sunlight, leaving a perfectly formed double rainbow. Rainbows are a common sight over Hobart. People all over town lift their bedroom blinds of a morning to check with the mountain what they should wear for the day: not a good plan, in fact, because it is forever changing its mind. In winter, it can disappear for days on end, as if it had never been there at all. In summer, its jagged profile is so sharp against the pale western sky it might have been cut from tissue paper.

As Tim Bowden remembers it, 'Our house in Sandy Bay faced north, and the mountain was a constant presence, regarded more with affection than apprehension – a more reliable weather indicator than our much-tapped barometer.'[3] In fact, Hobart's weather is notoriously difficult to predict, whatever method you use, and it is the mountain that helps to make it so. Neither the cold, capricious westerlies blowing off the Indian Ocean in winter and spring, nor the hot summer northerlies coming in from the Midlands are easy to second guess.

It is no exaggeration to say that human migration to Tasmania, and the way its societies developed, have largely depended on the weather. Some 20000 years ago, people living in more northerly parts of Australia were able to move here because an icy climate had lowered sea levels, exposing a land bridge across what is now Bass Strait. The last time anyone was able to walk into Tassie was about 10000 years ago. As a result of their subsequent isolation, Tasmanian Aboriginal societies developed their own unique characteristics: in effect, because of a change in the climate.

Europeans, on the other hand, were carried here by the strong westerlies. On his voyage to the southern continent, Tasman sailed down from Mauritius to 49 degrees south. Had he stayed at that latitude, he would have gone straight past the island without seeing it, but the weather was so bad and the seas so rough that he had to turn north. Consequently, on 24 November 1643, the moun-

tains of the island's west coast emerged through
late-afternoon mist and European interest in Tasmania flickered into life. The westerlies would
continue to blow new settlers in until the advent
of steamships began to lessen their influence. An
entire history of Tasmania could be told in terms
of people gradually freeing themselves from their
vulnerability to the weather.

People have been tapping barometers in Hobart
for a very long time. In fact, an observatory established here by the British government in 1840,
along with similar installations at Saint Helena
and the Cape of Good Hope, could be said to
have marked the beginnings of global meteorology.
Forecasting the weather was vital for shipping, and
data was soon being collated from lighthouses and
shore stations around Tasmania's coastline.

Although a good deal milder than they had
been used to back in England, Hobart's climate
was a big problem to the early settlers, huddled in
tents or shanties with only the light cotton clothing they had been issued with. In 1804, Lieutenant
Governor David Collins complained to his superi-
ors in London that, 'the winter season in this latitude is being severely felt by the People.'[4] Adequate
housing and clothing would solve the problem and

within a generation the weather had assumed a more benign reputation.

A reminder of early misconceptions about the local climate is a hefty brick perimeter wall at the Royal Botanical Gardens, built at the instigation of Lieutenant Governor George Arthur in 1829. It incorporates an ingenious ducted heating system fed by fireplaces at its base, intended to facilitate the growing of fruit trees and tender vegetables. It was hardly used, for the climate was soon found to be ideal for this purpose without any artificial stimulus. In fact, it is odd that it was ever felt to be necessary at all, for people had been extolling the mildness of Hobart's climate from the beginning. In 1823, Godwin's *Emigrant Guide to Van Diemen's Land* praised it in the highest terms as, 'perhaps, the most salubrious and congenial climate of any in the known world for an European constitution. It has been ascertained by the thermometer to be similar to that of the south of France.'[5] This was, and is, about right.

There are volumes of similar endorsements, Trollope, for example, declaring that, 'The climate of Tasmania is by far pleasanter than that of any part of the mainland. I found the summer weather of Hobart Town to be delicious. And there were no musquitoes there.'[6] Well, none that bit him anyway.

Trollope didn't stick around for winter. Yet other Englishmen who did were apparently not overly troubled by it. George Hull, an army man stationed in New South Wales, requested a transfer to Van Diemen's Land in 1819 because he couldn't stand Sydney's humidity. He made good use of Hobart's chilly winters by siring thirteen children.[7]

It didn't take long for the Tasmanian authorities to realise that Hobart's mild summers were a major attraction for overheated mainlanders swaddled in three-piece suits or many-layered petticoats. January in Melbourne could be no fun at all when the moral climate prevented you from getting your clothes off. Tasmanian tourism was sold to mainlanders mainly on the delights of its summer weather. In an early example of niche marketing, a different strategy was adopted for potential British immigrants, who were assured that, while Hobart had all the physical attributes of an English village, its winters were far more tolerable.

'COOL OFF IN TASMANIA', advises a 1930s travel poster, with a gent in a hat and overcoat surrounded by suitcases pointing triumphantly to a giant thermometer: 'Average temperature hottest month 62.3°' (16.8 degrees Celsius). Despite the statistical exactitude (which today's advertisers would regard as decidedly uncool), this hardly seems a sufficient inducement, but perhaps tourists then were more easily satisfied.

Then along came beach culture. A flash of leg or arm was no longer shameful, but sexy. Why cross Bass Strait when you could strip off at Bondi, Rosebud or Glenelg and splash about in the bracing sea? A fortnight in Hobart could do nothing for your tan. Thus Tassie lost its main attraction and took on a more fuddy-duddy image. It was only for those too old or too staid for the beach.

Fortunately, the setback was temporary. Today, with tans less fashionable and melanomas proliferating, lazing on the beach in the hot sun seems less like a good idea. With fears about global warming tarnishing the image of mainland summers, Tasmania's temperate climate has again become a selling point. (Changing popular attitudes to heat and cold would make a fascinating study in its own right.)

The problem is, of course, that temperate summers are not a year-round phenomenon. The tourist season in the late nineteenth century was acknowledged to be from January to around Easter, which was acceptable only so long as tourism was nobody's full-time occupation. Today, Hobart is inventing clever ways to sell its winters as well, with images of kiddies frolicking in the snow (the woollen beanie may be Tasmania's most representative fashion statement), happy couples sipping cocoa by roaring log fires, and the promise of generous off-season discounts. The annual Antarctic Midwinter Festival includes Polar Pathway Tours, the Longest Night Film Festival, a Huskies Picnic (where the huskies are an added attraction, not an item on the menu) and an Amundsen Afternoon Tea at Hadley's Hotel – a 'traditional Devonshire tea' followed by a visit to Hadley's 'gracious Amundsen Suite'. The irony is that when he turned up at Hadley's after his trip to the south pole in 1912, Roald Amundsen found the hotel less than gracious, confiding to his diary that he had been 'treated as a tramp' and given 'a miserable little room'. Time and tourism heal all wounds.

Local writer Bernard Lloyd, who is researching Hobart's Antarctic connections, recently rang Hadley's to book the Amundsen Suite. The helpful receptionist warned him that it was not the room Amundsen stayed in, merely one named in his honour. 'He was very scruffy', she said, 'and he arrived with his dogs. We almost threw him out!'

The 'we' is a nice touch, given that she was referring to events of nearly a century ago.

The bright orange icebreaker *Aurora Australis*, which ties up on Salamanca's doorstep on its regular home visits from the southern continent, provides a constant reminder that Hobart is the base for Australia's Antarctic operations. As the supply ship for Casey, Mawson and Davis bases, it takes everything from food and general supplies to aircraft parts and bulldozers, bringing back rubbish and other unwanted things. On the face of it, this does not seem to be a good bargain, but Hobart benefits financially from Commonwealth funding of the Australian Antarctic Division, and intellectually from the glaciologists, geologists, marine biologists and ornithologists who have taken up residence here (there are reputedly more natural scientists in Hobart, per capita, than in any other Australian city). So it is well worth collecting the Antarctic's rubbish. The *Aurora Australis* has a fully equipped laboratory on board, although that is less important now that researchers can fly directly to Mawson from Hobart.

Thus, an Antarctic Midwinter Festival does have some point to it, with the added bonus of making winter in Hobart seem like the tropics by comparison. Indeed, winters do have their particular ritualistic pleasures. You might expect the locals to be blasé about mountain snow. It is, after all, a common enough sight. But the first fall of the season always sends a ripple of childlike excitement through town. Bundling themselves up in thermals and ugh boots, normally sane, level-headed folk rush expectantly to the summit (or to the Springs, halfway up, if the snow cover is heavy enough to have closed the road), to hurl snowballs at anyone who comes within striking distance. Nobody copping an unexpected face-full of wet mush would dare spoil the collective fun by protesting: that would be to break an unwritten code. For this is carnival, a reversal of the usual rules, where physical assault on complete strangers is not only tolerated but encouraged. It's all completely pointless, of course, and the novelty wears off fairly quickly, but it gives Hobart people a chance to let their hair down while highlighting a point of difference between themselves and those in other Australian cities – 'This is something we can enjoy that you can't' – making it a social ritual of some significance. When you've thrown enough snow around and your feet are starting to get numb, it is customary to build a snowman on the bonnet of your car so you can race down into town before it melts. The safety implications hardly bear thinking about, but few accidents seem to result.

The chilly winters provide more than just an excuse for a bit of riotous behaviour in the snow, however. Generally speaking, Australians have an exaggerated fear of the cold. It doesn't fit with our bronzed-Aussie, sporty, outdoorsy self-image. It is just not fun. Sitting inside with the heater on is unmanly and effete, suggesting brain activity rather than the physical kind. Yet to those for whom brain activity is no embarrassment, the weather helps to concentrate the mind. Hobart's relatively cool climate contributes to its rich artistic, literary and intellectual life. Cool places are creative places, which is one reason the Enlightenment happened in Europe and not the Caribbean.

If you have come here from the tropics, however, you might be unimpressed. For some immigrants, winters are a real shock. 'Before you come you should be told that Tasmania is a very cold place, very cold,' complained one West African refugee. 'It is not good for someone that is afraid of cold. This state is really cold. It is freezing. So when someone is coming here you should be well prepared; if you are coming to Hobart, mentally prepared. It is very cold, this place.'[8]

On the other hand, one R Garvie of Lindisfarne wrote to the *Mercury* in the early 1960s, just as tourism was beginning to really take off, to caution that too much loose talk about the weather was bad for Tasmania's economy. It is an opinion that has often been expressed since. Mr or Ms Garvie, who clearly combined a rugged constitution with refined linguistic sensibility, declared that, 'The thin ephemeral morning rime that occasionally decorates our lawns and is described locally as "frost" is a pathetic imitation of the real thing.'[9]

Responses to the weather will always be highly subjective. Yet, despite R Garvie's insouciance, Hobart's average temperatures, both summer and winter, are undeniably lower than those of the other Australian capitals (except for Canberra, which is much colder in winter). The mean daily minimum for the coldest month, July, is 4.5 degrees Celsius, which, thanks to the moderating influence of the Tasman Sea, is not significantly lower than Melbourne's 5.8 degrees. In January, the hottest month, Melbourne and Sydney enjoy an average maximum of 25.8 degrees, Brisbane 29.4 and Hobart 21.5.

(This, you might have noticed, is a little higher than the 62.3 degrees Fahrenheit on the 1930s travel poster: not a sign of global warming but the vagaries of statistics-gathering, 62.3 degrees being the 24-hour daily average rather than the average maximum.)

Statistics cannot convey the whole story, however. Hobart's clean air, and the thinning ozone layer above it, make the sunshine here more intense than elsewhere in Australia. Actually, there is some dispute about this – meteorologists tend to pooh-pooh the idea – but everyone knows that, provided you stay in the sun, it will always feel a lot warmer than it officially is. The radiant heat seeps right into your bones. There is good reason for the fact that houses with north-facing windows are far more expensive than those without. In short, don't be fooled when the evening news tells you it will get to only 9 degrees tomorrow. If you stay in the sun and out of the breeze, you won't even need a jumper.

Your perception of the weather will also depend on what part of the city you are in. For instance, South Hobart, directly beneath the mountain, is noticeably cooler and wetter than Sandy Bay, a mere five or ten minutes away, and higher suburbs such as Fern Tree or Mount Nelson are much colder than both. Hobart has not one climate but many. This can make weather forecasts seem less reliable than they actually are. While people in Bellerive are scoffing that the predicted showers never came, those in West Hobart are wishing they would stop.

Any old Hobartian will tell you, however, that the climate now is very different from when they were kids. Summers are hotter, winters milder, and both are drier. We will never again see anything like the 1960 floods that inundated Liverpool Street and left hundreds homeless, nor the big snowfall of 1986, which allowed an enterprising show-off to ski to work across the Tasman Bridge.

Yet the reason people remember these events so vividly is that they were exceptional. Time has ironed out the endless days of no flood or snowfall. When an elderly man insists that climate change is real because he remembers shivering all day in the classroom, it is the school's inadequate heating he is calling to mind. Today we have adjusted to being artificially warmed wherever we go, but outside it is pretty much as it was.

Nor has climate change caused more bushfires. There are just more misfits with kerosene and matches lighting them. So far, at least, climate change appears to have had less impact on Tasmania than on other parts of Australia.

'It is slightly warmer and drier in Tasmania now than it was a hundred years ago,' says the Bureau of Meteorology's public officer, Malcolm Riley, 'and we have less snow events, but the changes are minimal. In terms of temperature we are looking at a change of only fractions of a degree.'[10]

One statistic that every tour guide likes to quote, because it is guaranteed to astonish, is that Hobart is, on average, Australia's second-driest capital. Its average yearly rainfall of 624 millimetres exceeds only Adelaide's 555. Both Canberra and Melbourne are wetter. By the time the westerlies roar over Mount Wellington and down into Collins Street, most of their moisture has long since been extracted. Charles Darwin found Hobart a lush, green place with delightful English-style gardens but the locals could have told him that he had chanced upon an unusually wet summer. Casual observation, no matter how acute, can be an unreliable guide.

Very occasionally, in winter – perhaps only once every couple of years – at any hour of the night, telephones will ring across the city as people alert each other to the appearance of that most awe-inspiring of natural pageants: an aurora. While they can occur over many places in southern Australia, in Hobart and along Tasmania's east coast auroras are more vivid and your chances of seeing one are greater – around one or two per cent, according to the experts, on any clear winter's night. Whole families will stand shivering in dressing-gowns at their front gates or leap into their cars to join the conga-line heading to Mount Wellington's sum-mit for a clearer view. Nothing can quite prepare you for this eerily silent ballet of electronically-charged particles tossed by solar winds. Waves of colour billow across the southern sky from hori-zon to zenith like immense curtains, sometimes pierced by searchlight-shafts of green or red or framed by shimmering rainbow arches. Sydney's New Year's fireworks – mere contrivance – cannot compare. That auroras (at least those spectacular enough to get out of bed for) are infrequent and unpredictable only adds to their mysterious allure, although the secret of those people who get to the telephone first is that they have picked up an

Aurora Alert from the Australian Space Weather Agency's website.

As one overwhelmed observer said, somewhat ambiguously, about an aurora in October 2007, 'It's worth living in Hobart just for this!'

Bad behaviour

That early Hobart was a hotbed of crime should come as no surprise, given that the whole place was an open-air prison. The few honest souls with drive and ambition who, with convict labour, succeeded as farmers, merchants or shipowners, contributed a modicum of civility, but they could not expect much thanks. This was not, by anyone's standards, a normal society. Nor did the authorities in Britain have any interest in allowing it to become one. They had not paid a fortune to set up a penal colony only to see it degenerate into a comfortable and prosperous community. It was vital that felons sentenced to be transported to Van Diemen's Land be filled with horror at the prospect.

Indeed, Lieutenant Governor George Arthur arrived in 1824 with express orders to make sure of it. To this unforgiving martinet, criminals were the colony's *raison d'être*, free settlers merely 'Visitors'.

Meticulous records – a legacy of Arthur's military mindset – show that, in 1828 alone, just over nine per cent of all Tasmanians were convicted of drunkenness and nearly half of all convicts charged with a misdemeanour. Capital crimes, such as murder, bushranging, livestock theft and housebreaking, were also much more prevalent here than in New South Wales.[1]

Convicts and ex-convicts were not the only tormentors of decent folk. Whaling crews at a bit of a loss between slaughters made merry hell in the hundreds of pubs, dance halls, lodging houses and gambling dens around the waterfront. 'It is not to be tolerated', thundered the *Colonial Times* in 1839, 'that a mob of inebriated fools are to be permitted to march through the metropolis, assault the guardians of public peace, and disturb the quiet of the peaceable inhabitants with impunity.'[2]

What did the paper expect? Even the so-called peaceable inhabitants were hardly blameless. With class distinctions so fluid in the colony's early years, any uneducated free man or ex-convict could, with hard work and a bit of luck, rise to social prominence, but leaving behind his rough-and-tumble habits was another matter altogether. An easy familiarity with the manners and moral codes of society is not something that can just be picked up. It takes a generation or two to be absorbed. Therefore, the newly rich in Hobart Town were invariably the vulgar rich. Violence and decorum went hand in hand.

The wealthy whaling tycoon James Kelly, for instance (after whom Kelly Steps at Salamanca Place are named), was, in later life, a respectable family man and a pillar of society, with a fine stone house. He was also a violent thug, charged on more than one occasion with brawling in the streets. It was not unusual for the most prominent citizens to openly engage in criminal or at least unruly behaviour.[3] These days, they have learnt to be more discreet.

In a society full of petty thieves, lowlifes and chancers, allowances had to be made. Free settlers battled on, not only against dishonest businessmen, politicians, convicts and emancipists, whose wickedness was only to be expected, but also against disgruntled soldiers, who were no less likely to offend than those they were supposed to be keeping under control.

No wonder, then, that the minority who considered themselves 'society' over-reacted, developing a prissy, self-protective attitude to any social peccadillo. In the 1840s Louisa Anne Meredith observed approvingly that:

> Not in the most moral circles of moral England herself is a departure from the paths of propriety or virtue more determinedly or universally visited by the punishment of exclusion from society, than in this 'Penal Colony'; nowhere are all particulars and incidents of persons' past lives more minutely and rigidly canvassed, than in the 'higher circles' of this little community; and nowhere are the decent and becoming observances of social and domestic life more strictly maintained.[4]

By this time, the rough edges of George Arthur's military establishment were being smoothed out under the enlightened patronage of Sir John and Lady Franklin, who believed that education and the arts were better than whips and chains for the reform of wrongdoers. It was a delightful fantasy – for the few it embraced – but its effect was to widen the social gap. 'Franklin's "Hobarton" was a strangely exotic growth within a savage landscape,' writes Peter Bolger; 'the unspeakable existing alongside eloquence.'[5]

Around the time Louisa was delighting in the fact that Hobart's streets were safer for an unaccompanied lady than those of an English village, a less sanguine English visitor wailed that 'in the streets it is as common a thing to see females as males reeling in all the filth of beastly drunkenness, and blasphemy most horrible ...'[6] It all depended upon which side of the social divide you found yourself on: the Englishman, William Gates, was talking about the wharf area at night, while Louisa lived in genteel New Town, with its neat stone houses and pretty gardens, where she mixed with other ladies of quality, serenely unfazed by the brutalities around her.

Not until the early 1850s, with transportation ended, self-government achieved and civil law established in place of the old military codes, did cases of physical assault, property crime and disorderly conduct begin to fall. But the fall was dramatic. In the 1860s Hobart had one of the highest crime rates in Australia: by the 1880s it had one of the lowest.[7] There were several reasons for this.

For one thing, the riches that flowed from gold fever on the mainland (later backed up by lucrative exports of wool and minerals) brought new optimism and confidence. The 'cesspit of the empire', as *The Times* in London had so cruelly labelled it not a decade earlier, suddenly found itself, in the joyful words of a contemporary novelist, 'disgustingly rich' – although he might have been getting a bit carried away. As a result, the proportion of women and children dramatically increased. For the first time, young people outnumbered the old and dissipated. Meanwhile, emancipated convicts, especially older ones who had been the major committers of crimes, left in droves to take their chances in Ballarat or Bendigo, where they could try to free themselves of their pasts. Either that or they died.

Aside from a brief but savage recession in the 1860s, Hobart was a good place for the average worker in the latter part of the nineteenth century. Wages and working conditions were better than they were in England at that time and any man with a bit of initiative could provide well for his family. As the baleful influence of the old convict class gradually ebbed away, the influx of skilled workers increased. Meanwhile, the native-born, proud of their island home and fiercely protective of its reputation, were keen to break with its sordid history, to put all that behind them and look to the future. Hobart's sunny prospects provided a strong inducement to uprightness.

Thus, when the government's indefatigable statistician, RM Johnston, published his *Tasmanian Official Record* in 1892, he took great satisfaction in showing that rates of property crime and assault in Hobart were lower than in Britain or in any other of the Australian colonies, even those that had never had substantial numbers of convicts. Furthermore, he boasted, the good folk of Hobart were only half as likely as their Melbourne or Sydney counterparts to witness drunken violence on the streets. Johnston had good reason to be pleased: it had been a remarkable turnaround.

Despite − or partly because of − the catastrophic depressions of the 1890s and 1930s, and the shadows of two world wars, crime rates remained remarkably stable until the 1950s. The foundations of a settled civil society had been well laid. While honest folk may still have fretted about violence or theft, they saw it as a blight on their fundamentally respectable society, not, as they would have a century or so earlier, a visible symptom of pervasive rottenness. Crime was inevitable, but manageable.

Sharp dips in convictions for assault during both world wars suggest that, in difficult times, an insular society pulls together. Internal disruptions are more than usually unacceptable in the face of outside threat. To guilt is added shame, especially when everyone knows everyone.

Yet the twentieth century brought a new and very troubling trend, which also played its part. As we have seen, it was no longer the old and unwanted leaving the colony, but the young, fit and talented. Some went off to war, many left to find work on the mainland. If crime rates remained stable, therefore, depopulation, and the apathy, truculence and despondency of those who remained had their part to play in it. Few had the energy for unruliness. The fires had gone out.

Accordingly – and paradoxically, given past experiences – when things started looking up in the 1950s, crime rates began to increase, for the first time in over half a century, peaking about twenty years later.[8] Although drugs had nothing like the impact they had on the mainland during this period, they did contribute to the incidence of property crime, public order offences and petty theft, as well as creating some new categories of criminal behaviour that hadn't existed previously. Young people, like their counterparts of a hundred years earlier, wanted to put the past behind them, only this time they were motivated not by pride in their island home, but disdain for their parents' generation. Their rebellion took a different and more solipsistic form.

With the old lags long since passed into history, it was now mostly young males committing the assaults, property offences and 'outrages against common decency'. And so it remains today.

Young men get a bad press because their anti-social behaviour is most likely to personally affect other people. A drunken fight in the mall is an event. It raises the heat, feeding the newspapers a lurid headline or two. A businessman fiddling the books or a politician caught lying, on the other hand, will provoke cynical fascination rather than personal fear (and is less likely to be exposed in the first place). That has always been the case, with Tasmania consistently providing lots of high-level corruption to be cynically fascinated by.

In this relatively safe and, some would say, sleepy city, most people's personal experience of crime is limited to unruly behaviour fuelled by testosterone and alcohol. Although that sort of thing has always alarmed decent citizens, today, with high-powered cars in the mix, it is a lot more threatening.

In the 1960s, 'Apprehensive' wrote to the *Mercury* demanding that law-abiding people be given 'some protection from "hooliganism" which is running rampant in our city and elsewhere. There should be a campaign for the birch for these morons.'[9] Today, some forty or more years later, those same hooligans who upset Apprehensive will themselves be sitting in their recliner chairs muttering angrily into their cocoa about a new generation of young thugs. And so it goes around.

Those thugs are largely the product of a social divide that pits the newer suburbs of the Eastern Shore against the more established ones on the city side of the river (the fact that it is never referred to as 'the western shore' being an indication of who makes the distinctions).

'We have pockets of residential areas which are neglected,' says Acting Assistant Commissioner of Police, Steve Bonde, 'but we don't have real slums. All the areas with houses over a hundred years old are now desirable places to live. Our problem areas are those between ten and twenty years old.' In this respect, Hobart differs from many other cities, where it is older neighbourhoods that breed crime.

> What happens with a Housing Department area
> [says Bonde], is that when it first kicks off there
> are lots of young families, so it's lovely for a
> few years. Then the kids become teenagers and

it starts to go downhill. Later it progresses to personal ownership of the houses: the government tends to sell the houses to occupants who want to buy them. So for the next twenty years it starts to improve as people start to take pride in their places … and the crime rate goes down. We've got lots of suburbs in Hobart that have been through that process.

Rokeby, on the Eastern Shore, is one. It is currently undergoing the transition to private home-ownership – the third stage in Steve Bonde's progression towards respectability. Yet not everything is rosy in Rokeby.

Mick (not his real name) is a recovering alcoholic who lives there in a government-owned house with his school-aged daughter. He has a labouring job, his first in a long time, and is 'getting his life together', mainly for his daughter's sake. But the neighbourhood, he says, isn't helping. 'Our neighbours are scum, and half the kids I went to school with are either dead or in jail … You've got stolen cars doing wheelies every night and the house next door to my ex-wife's was shot at from a car a few weeks ago. It makes me angry', he says, 'that there's no police after five o'clock. The local station shuts down. The cops have given up on us.' Perhaps he is exaggerating — all suburban police stations close at night — but his distress is real enough.

All the same, Mick has no intention of moving. 'I was brought up here. I know everyone. I can't imagine living anywhere else. I'm not involved in drugs and I've given up on the booze, so I'm okay here.' Whatever the disadvantages, people prefer to stick with what they know. Perhaps it's loyalty to places and friends, perhaps it's just a lack of initiative.

Of more concern to the police is neighbouring Clarendon Vale. Belying its pretty name and its peaceful, semi-rural setting, Clarendon Vale is 'shocking', according to the acting assistant commissioner:

> It's gone past the stage of being new and relatively quiet to being a real melting pot ... Almost all our stolen motor vehicles end up down there burning on the fringes of the bush. We have assaults on the street. It would be comparable with, say, Macquarie Plains in Sydney. We've never had those sorts of riots, of course, but the community I saw on television at the time of those riots is very like that of Clarendon Vale or

Gagebrook. The difference is that they are much smaller: 500 homes instead of 5000.

Winemaker Dirk Meure, formerly a lawyer and lecturer in law at the University of Tasmania, points out that most of Hobart's serious crime can be traced to a handful of families, who go on offending through successive generations:

When I was working at Risdon [Prison] in the late sixties and early seventies, there were parts of North Hobart, specific streets, which were the slums where the families of people in prison lived. Now they would be living around Gagebrook and those areas ... I'm sure if I went back to the jail now after thirty or so years, I'd be able to see the same families represented there. If your dad has been to jail, you're likely to [go] as well, because the system produces its own criminals. It's not some bad gene. When I was a criminal lawyer, I knew a father with seven kids. He stole some potatoes, the magistrate sentenced him to nine months. That means his family was now on welfare, all his kids were the sons of a crim. When he got out of jail he couldn't get a job. So they've all become part of the system. It's not just the individual being punished. There's an amazing social impact.

Criminal records in Tasmania are remarkably thorough, going right back to [Lieutenant Governor] Arthur's day. We have a very clear, long-term record of criminal patterns in families. The people doing the recording are those working in the system and keeping it going, so there's a feedback loop ... What criminologists used to call secondary deviance is amplified by workers in the field knowing these families, keeping an eye on them and so on, so it becomes almost a self-fulfilling prophesy. This is not unique to Tasmania, but what is unique is that it's all documented so well.

Immigrants, especially Asians and black Africans, tell stories of verbal and physical abuse on buses, in shops and on the street. People who look different are an obvious and easy target. Sometimes eggs or plastic bottles are thrown, hijabs are pulled off, and so on, although only rarely is real physical injury caused. The abusers are almost always young males and, with a predictable lack of imagination, they almost always shout, 'Go back to where you came from!' Many have absorbed the common wisdom that immigrants are taking their jobs, despite there being no evidence for that. There is, however, evidence that refugees are exacerbating an already dire public-housing shortage, although they can hardly be blamed for that.

One young woman from Central Africa reported: 'We went shopping and we were outside putting the food in the car and they threw a bottle of water at us from their car and they shouted, "Take these people back to their own country".'[10] Although not the sort of incident the police are likely to respond to, it is frightening for people already traumatised by war, famine and disruption.

In Tasmania, complains a man from West Africa,

> ... the black people face problems that the
> white people do not face here. I'm talking about
> discrimination ... There are certain areas when
> you pass, it is mostly younger guys, when you
> walk in they shout at you, they call you certain
> names. This is not physical, but it is insulting
> violence. I think it has increased. One time I was
> riding a bicycle, I reached the traffic lights, when
> the lights came on I was going to go and this car
> drove past and said, 'You f'ing black monkey,
> what are you doing here?'[11]

More disturbing, because more premeditated, are attacks on immigrants' houses: bricks thrown through windows, slogans daubed on walls, and gardens laid waste. This slow war of attrition will continue until the irritants are driven away and normality is restored. All public housing tenants, whether immigrant or not, are vulnerable to harassment in their houses. They are seen as lazy opportunists living off the hard-working taxpayer. Africans and Asians suffer more not only because they stand out, but because they are few in number and widely dispersed. In bigger cities, ethnic minorities can band together for protection and support. Unfortunately, that can lead to gang warfare among ethnic groups of the kind that has blighted some areas of Melbourne and Sydney, but the smallness of immigrant populations and relatively low social pressures make that unlikely here.

Contrary to what the West African man quoted above might think, racial abuse is no worse in Hobart than anywhere else, nor is it increasing. In fact the reverse is almost certainly true, although comparative figures are not available.

He is also incorrect in thinking that white people are free from discrimination. A top hat can be no less of a provocation than a hijab. In November

2007, the *Mercury* reported that a teenage victim of
serial bullying had been bashed unconscious in the
Elizabeth Street Mall. 'Three girls [who witnessed
the attack] said he was constantly picked on for
wearing a "Willie-Wonka"-style purple top hat.
The boy is about seventeen. "I'm used to people
picking on me", he said.'[12] His real offence was
his playful disrespect for convention, which can
be very confronting to the insecure. Traditionally,
Hobart has been a haven for social conformity, so
any non-conforming behaviour stands out. That is
changing, but slowly.

Long-running subculture rivalries were blamed
for three separate assaults on teenagers just before
Christmas 2007. 'It's a territory thing', explained
one of the young victims. He blamed Eastern
Shore bogans who target 'those from the alternative scene, such as Emos and Goths ... It's the conservative versus the avant-garde',[13] he added, as if
being bashed in the street was confirmation of his
progressiveness.

Yet how representative are incidents such as
these? The media, whose job it is to instil fear,
report them with relish, so people naturally look
on the mall and Franklin Square as dangerous. Statistically, however, Hobart's streets remain the safest

of any capital city's, just as they were in the early 1890s.

> I like to go for a walk before bed [says Steve Bonde], and I can think of only a couple of areas of about five or six hundred square metres of Hobart that I wouldn't walk around at night ... The Australian Bureau of Statistics figures show us to be lower on the national scale for all crime categories ...

He concedes that the mall and Franklin Square can be rowdy, even a bit threatening at times:

> Young people gather there and swear and drop skateboards onto the pavement with a clatter ... There are occasionally fights, especially over girls, and there is also some territory involved, although we do our best not to let anyone claim any territory ... But our reported crime figures tell us that those are not problem areas at all, so the public perception is really quite mistaken ... It's loutishness rather than crime, but there's quite a bit of it. They mean no harm to anybody, they just get a bit loud and they can be concerning to the elderly and infirm ... From a policing perspective, I'd prefer them to be in a place where we're going to be spending a lot of time rather

than in a park at the top end of Davey Street or something where it's more difficult to keep an eye on them.

Today the Hobart region has one police officer for every 468 people: the highest ratio in Australia apart from the Northern Territory. Some – politicians foremost among them – point to this as the reason for low crime rates. Others, taking into consideration the various social and cultural factors that help to keep Hobart safe, question whether the high numbers of police, and the considerable public resources invested in them, are really necessary.

Bullying is not, of course, the sole preserve of the lawless. The law itself is more than capable of it, as any gay man of a certain age will tell you. In the 1970s and 1980s, with Sydney's Oxford Street in full swing and advertisers eagerly latching on to the 'pink dollar', Tasmanian homosexuals still cowered under constant threat of punishment. Needless to say, Hobart had no gay venues, just an informal social group which convened occasionally, each time at a different location to avoid the attentions of the police, who would turn up anyway to ostentatiously note down car registration numbers. The authorities were said to keep a 'pink list' on which the names of some very prominent citizens were recorded. Whether it actually existed, and whether it was ever used for blackmail, is debatable, but people *believed* it did and that was what mattered.

Gays were faced with a simple choice: leave the state and be free or stay and be hounded. Many left, but those who stayed did so for economic or family reasons or because of an emotional attachment to the place of their birth, however shoddily their loyalty was repaid.

'A group of us decided we were unhappy with those two choices', says Rodney Croome. 'In 1988 we set up a card-table at Salamanca Market, between Amnesty International and the Greens, to hand out leaflets calling for the law to be changed. But we underestimated the ferocity of the response.'

The council banned the stall as incompatible with the 'family nature of the market', and when the ban was ignored, as everyone knew it would be, the arrests began: 130 of them over about a dozen successive Saturdays. 'I was arrested for being gay long before I'd so much as danced with another man', says Rodney. 'Even petitioning to have the laws rescinded was illegal.'

Max Burr, MHA for Lyons, declared that homosexuals should hang their heads in shame for bringing AIDS into the world. The Reverend John McRae of Sandy Bay Uniting Church, with the lofty condescension of those who have the truth on their side, insisted that homosexuals should be forgiven, although for what, exactly, he didn't say. In any case, few of the outraged citizens who wrote to the *Mercury* were in a forgiving mood, one declaring that AIDS was 'a blessing in disguise' that 'will help rid the world of these creatures.'[14] Robin Gray's state Liberal government, apparently keen to hasten the process, helpfully added an AIDS Council safe-sex pamphlet to its restricted publications list.

When the laws were finally changed in 1997, thanks in no small part to then state Attorney General Judy Jackson (who, as a Labor MHA, had been one of the few state politicians with the courage to oppose the Salamanca Market arrests) they changed radically. It was as if years of dammed-up guilt, going right back to convict days, had finally been flushed out.

Today, same-sex partners are encouraged to register their relationships and they enjoy equal status under the law. Out in suburbia, all those outraged mothers of three have learned to keep their opinions to themselves. In November 2008 the Hobart City Council, which had so tenaciously organised the arrests just twenty years earlier, marked the anniversary with a civic reception for what it now calls 'the gay community'. It is a turnaround of official attitude so astonishing as to seem unnatural: just one manifestation of a fundamental shift in the self-image of local authorities from the stern and somewhat lofty law-makers of a generation ago to benign friends of the people, accommodating to all and anxious to avoid offence.

Keeping occupied

A young man venting his spleen in the *Mercury*'s letters pages in 2005 called Hobart 'boring. There is not much to do and everything is closed on weekends.' Another concurred: 'it's no wonder that young and talented people leave this state in droves.'[1] There is no use in pointing out to such people that their frustration might be the result of their own lack of imagination: the sentiment is shared by many who long for release. For the insecure young in particular, release means losing yourself, and Hobart does not make that easy. Like small cities and towns everywhere, it throws you back on your own resources. The unresourceful inevitably get bored.

The vast majority of people are content to be consumers of ready-made entertainments and cultural trends from overseas, sitting back to absorb whatever comes their way. And what comes their way is American mass-culture. In pubs and clubs all over Hobart, bands are appropriating American accents to sing American songs; conversations around office water-coolers centre on *Batman Regurgitated* or last night's episode of *CSI Miami*; and, at Salamanca on Saturday nights, revellers who want to be cool adopt the American idiom. Even their body language – their 'attitude', to use the American expression – has been picked up from the movies.

It is no wonder, then, that to these people Hobart feels a bit like Hippo Regius must have during the heyday of the Roman Empire: a backwater, remote from the action, with no hope of catching up. Mass consumption of overseas entertainment, delivered in an instant electronically, can only reinforce that sense of isolation, irrelevance and second-rateness. Globalised entertainment networks are designed to put the peripheral in their place.

The distinction often made between popular and high cultures might more usefully be thought of in a place like this as one between a culture that rejoices in American hegemony and a regionalist one that – often ineffectually – asserts pride in the home-grown. That distinction, however, is not always clear-cut.

Nowhere is it more playfully enacted than at a bar called Joe's Garage in Wapping, behind City Hall: a cleverly devised hybrid of an Australian outback mechanic's shed and an American truck-stop diner. In the deserted backstreets of Hobart, it could hardly look more out of place, but that is, of course, the attraction for the bearded blokes in blue jeans and plaid shirts who hover around their Harleys and Hondas outside. Well-dressed Theatre Royal patrons, returning to the carpark next door after a performance of *Macbeth* or a David William-son play, maintain a wary distance.

Joe's Garage resurrects, in a more knowing and self-ironising guise, the kind of rough and rowdy drinking establishments that crammed this now otherwise genteel area in the nineteenth century. Whereas Joe's Garage pays homage to America, they perpetuated Irish and English pub cultures. The crucial difference is that, in the early days at least, Hobart pubs were blind to social class. 'The freedom of all ranks of society, including con-victs and soldiers, to visit pubs – virtually unre-stricted until the mid-1820s – is one of the most remarkable aspects of early Van Diemen's Land', writes James Boyce.

Until the evening curfew (in Hobart Town in
1820 this was eight o'clock in winter and nine
o'clock in summer), ordinary Van Diemonians
– male and female, bonded and free, sailor and
settler, policeman and prisoner – got drunk
together, usually on rum imported from India.
There were 11 pubs in Hobart Town by 1818 ...[2]

By the latter half of the nineteenth century,
drinkers had, broadly speaking, divided into two
classes. The rough and poor were restricted to non-
commercial and non-residential districts such
as Goulburn Street and upper Macquarie Street,
where the police were less likely to bother them.
The middle-class 'Gingers', so-called, caroused in
the more respectable areas, flaunting their wealth
and irresponsibility. The police didn't bother
them much either, so it was claimed, because they
had enough influence to be able to come to some
arrangement. 'Hobart is ... a town of taverns,
some of high degree and others of very low degree
indeed,' noted a contemporary commentator:

All around these places was much poverty and
wickedness. From six o'clock in the morning until
midnight the liquor was sold to vicious men and
squalid and dissipated women. The better class

of hotels in the principal streets did not go in for this sort of thing. They catered for the flourishing middle class, and when the house was popular the licensee did a big business.[3]

Today, when people are more socially and geographically mobile, those class distinctions have again melted away. Salamanca Place, the city's current eating and drinking area of choice, presents an egalitarian mix of young and old, rich and poor, sophisticated and rowdy, diners and boozers and those just out for a stroll and a look about.

As cafe culture has gradually usurped the old pub culture, local hotels, faced with falling patronage, have had to diversify, since only a few have gaming machine licences. The races on Sky Channel will no longer suffice. Bistros, cocktail lounges and family areas are now minimum requirements. Even a name-change is worth a try. The Empire in North Hobart has blossomed since it morphed into the Republic (a ghostly residue of the original name survives on the parapet as a reminder of its constitutional about-face). The new name reflects a radically different image: dinners, local jazz and rock bands, poetry readings, art exhibitions, debates, and political gatherings of a leftish-greenish tinge. There is something endearingly sixties about the Republic: local, ideological and communal, with an air of self-conscious bohemianism. You go there not just to imbibe and be entertained, but to declare your allegiances. It is the equivalent of the Tasmanian Club for people who wouldn't be seen dead in the Tasmanian Club (and would never be allowed in anyway).

'Pub culture is extremely important to the contemporary music industry', says David Williams, the editor of *Sauce*, Tasmania's free gig guide. 'Outside of music festivals, almost all contemporary music performance happens in pubs. Alcohol sales provide the money for licensees to spend on entertainment, and entertainment draws people in to purchase alcohol. It's a two-way process: almost a symbiotic relationship.'

David is dismissive of complaints about boring old Hobart:

> Naturally Melbourne has more going on because there are more people: simple as that. Bigger audiences, as well as more people to take financial risks in putting on entertainment. But there's more going on in Hobart than young people realise: as much, or possibly even more than in Melbourne, per head of population. It's part of youth culture to be critical without being

sure of what they're criticising. The ones who
whinge about nothing going on are often the
ones who don't turn up when there is. This is an
entertainment *industry*. It's about people making a
living. So it has got to be supported.

Musicians, he says, are probably less constrained
by Hobart's geographical isolation than other artists are.

In industry terms, Tasmania is just not isolated
any more. You can build your career by posting
your music on YouTube or MySpace. The
problem used to be distribution, but not now.
There's a duo here called Scientists of Modern
Music who were signed up to a subsidiary of
EMI from Hobart after being promoted directly
to the labels by their manager.

Entertainers who have outgrown the pub circuit
can be accommodated at Wrest Point casino, where
the audience is made to sit on stacking chairs and
buy drinks at interval from a trestle table with a
cloth thrown over it; or at the barn-like Derwent
Entertainment Centre – capacity 7500 – designed
for everything from Silverchair and the Ten Tenors
to the Telstra Roadwalking Championships and the
National Careers and Employment Expo, which, of

course, makes it unsuited to anything in particular.

Chris Pearce remembers that, in the 1960s:

> Hobart was on the circuit for music. Johnny
> Cash came here, Fabian, the Beach Boys, Manfred
> Mann. I don't know why they all came, but they
> did. And there was always a lively jazz scene here.
> Other than that it was pretty quiet.

Nobody seems to know why the big names visit less often nowadays. Perhaps they've heard about the casino and the Entertainment Centre.

No stacking chairs for racegoers, meanwhile, for whom the new grandstand at Elwick Racecourse, a pet project of the sports-mad former premier Paul Lennon, provides every luxury. Footy fans are also well catered for, the state government having blown more than $15 million convincing a Melbourne AFL team to print the word 'Tasmania' on its jumpers. The state government pays lip service to cultural pursuits but a quick look around Hobart's cultural and entertainment infrastructure reveals the hollowness of the rhetoric.

At least the Tasmanian Symphony Orchestra has a suitable venue. The Federation Concert Hall is not without its critics — fewer since early 2009 when the acoustics were improved — but most agree it is perfectly serviceable. On the outside, its copper-sheathed cylindrical form gives a knowing postmodernist nod to the gasometers that dominated this area in its industrial days.

The Tasmanian Symphony Orchestra, which celebrated its sixtieth birthday in 2008, is a testament to the benefits of Federalism. Simply on grounds of fairness, the ABC's mandate to establish 'groups of musicians for the rendition of orchestral, choral and band music of high quality' in each state had to include Tasmania, despite the fact that its small population seemed hardly to warrant the expense. (Hobart city had fewer than 60 000 people in 1948.) A large metropolis could claim a symphony orchestra as its due – as a confident declaration of cultural maturity. For Hobart, however, such things are manna from heaven. As a result, the TSO has always enjoyed a special place in the hearts of grateful Tasmanians. The bond was amply demonstrated when the Federal Government's Review of Orchestras in 2005, looking for ways to cut costs, recommended that it be reduced to the size of a chamber orchestra. As things stand, the cost of maintaining it exceeds the entire annual state arts budget, which says more about the arts budget than the cost of the orchestra. The response, even from those who had never set foot in the Federation Concert Hall, was furious. Tasmania would not settle for a 'downgraded' orchestra (what might Richard Tognetti of the Australian Chamber Orchestra have said about that?). On the face of it, a chamber orchestra would suit Tasmania very well, if only because, being less expensive, it could be more adventurous in its programming and more mobile. However, the argument was not about music so much as state pride – a matter of some importance to Tasmanians – and it would be a brave politician prepared to take that on. The orchestra survived the fracas better funded and better patronised than before.

Those who see nothing wrong with music-making on an intimate scale can always try Musica Viva at the Town Hall (for which the dreaded stacking chairs must also be wheeled out) or they can catch some Boulez or Brett Dean at the Conservatorium's occasional recitals, where an encouragingly large proportion of the (admittedly modest) audience is likely to be under thirty-five years old. These are not the young contemporary music fans that magazines like *Sauce* are interested in.

It is to be hoped that the proposed new recital hall, to be built next to the Theatre Royal as part of the University of Tasmania's new Academy of Creative Industries and Performing Arts, will at last provide a suitable home for small-scale musical events in Hobart.

A wide range of options is what makes music such a strong force in Tasmania: it has what managerial types these days call 'an ecology', meaning a hierarchical network with major organisations at the top of the pyramid and a range of others – including specialised educational institutions – providing a foundation. This is not so much the case for live theatre, however.

For a city with the oldest theatre in Australia, and by far the prettiest, Hobart has not had a good run with professional performing companies. The Tasmanian Theatre Company, established with great fanfare in 2008, clings to life, despite losing all its government funding in 2012. An earlier company, Zootango, folded for lack of funds in 1997.

'Theatre is collaborative and expensive,' says Tim Munro, the Theatre Royal's Chief Executive:

> The new Tasmanian Theatre Company is a fairly modest operation. It uses the Backspace Theatre [behind the Theatre Royal] because it's a more sympathetic space for contemporary work. You can do more adventurous things there. It is not all

that suited to major productions, though, because with 150 seats you can't make them viable. It costs at least $50 000 to $100 000 to get a small local production up, and there's a long gestation period of up to three years, including the writing. But the idea is that the new company will build a subscriber base, develop a following and work up from there.

Tim Munro's optimism about the future of theatre in Tasmania is borne out by the fact that ticket sales at the Theatre Royal increased from 42 000 in 2004 to 67 000 in 2008. Hobart is big enough to support a live theatre 'ecology', and a strong, well-funded state company with its own home will, he maintains, create the necessary focus:

> We have a good repertory company in Hobart, with its own permanent venue, which, although it doesn't feed directly into the professional sphere, does encourage interest and participation. And we have excellent training: at Rosny, Hobart and Elizabeth Colleges at the secondary level and tertiary training at the University in Launceston. Students then have to go on to NIDA [National Institute of Dramatic Art in Sydney] or the VCA [Victorian College

of Arts in Melbourne] or other interstate
institutions to complete their studies. The trick
is to create an industry here for those students
to come back to.

In earlier times, people made their own entertainments, not all of which involved getting drunk. A
picnic was always a welcome weekend diversion.
Hobart was, and remains, the perfect city for a
picnic, with perhaps a leisurely walk in the bush
to follow. What little social life people otherwise
enjoyed generally revolved around the local church.
For the socially conscious, observing the Sabbath
was almost obligatory, and the churches wielded
considerable social power. Merely by playing any
sort of organised sport, joining a youth group,
or going to a Saturday night dance — even just by
attending school — chances are you were benefiting
from the self-interested generosity of a Christian
institution.

The church hall and the council-owned public
hall, which sat empty for most of the week apart
from the occasional stamp-collectors' or field-
naturalists' meeting, would burst into life at week-

ends for dances, concerts, flower shows and, from the early 1920s, picture shows. Anyone who could play an instrument would be roped in to provide music for Saturday night waltzes, square dances and barn dances. Groups of excited young people dressed to the nines, the girls bearing supper plates draped with tea towels, arrived by foot, sometimes from miles away, then walked home again, a little more subdued, when it was all over (or when father had decreed they must).

To earn his fare to the mainland, Max Angus played in a band at the Belvedere:

> It was at the bottom of Argyle Street, above a
> car showroom. We had an orchestra of twelve
> that played there Saturday nights. Men had to
> wear evening dress or navy blue, women in long
> evening dress. And we in the band wore bow
> ties. For those who liked dancing, it was the big
> entertainment on a Saturday night. We got 17/6d
> to play from eight-thirty to midnight or one in
> the morning.

Everyone loved dancing and Hobart had an extraordinary number of venues. Rob Valentine, who keeps lists of such things always at hand on his BlackBerry, can reel off dozens of them:

There was a big dance hall in the basement
under the Bank Arcade; one above McCann's; the
Trocadero, opposite the GPO; the Dugout; the
Stage Door, which was nicknamed the Snakepit;
the Sapphire Ballroom in Liverpool Street; the
Belvedere in Argyle Street; and the Continental
in Macquarie Street, opposite St Joseph's. The
Naval Ball used to be held at the HMAS *Huon*;
there were regular RSL balls, the Queen Mary
Club had dances in the forties; the Lord Mayor's
Courtroom here in the Town Hall was used for
old-time dancing classes and the Town Hall itself
was the venue for the Jazz House in 1956 and
'57. There were debutantes' and bachelors' balls
in the City Hall; Red Cross balls; Catholic and
Masonic balls; the spinsters' ball; an artists' ball;
autumn and spring balls and the Derwent Rowing
Club balls.

Television and rock 'n 'roll helped to kill them off.
Today, we are left with bobbing up and down at
nightclubs and footy socials fuelled by alcohol and
soundtracked electronically.

Government House boasts the city's most spectacular ballroom: nobly proportioned, with crystal
chandeliers, Huon pine floor, vaulted Gothic ceil-

ing and minstrel gallery. It is the crowning glory of what Trollope called the best government house belonging to any British colony. But no ball has been held there since Prince Charles insisted on one while visiting in the 1970s.

In 1956, the year television was introduced, the Blue Moon Cabaret, above shops in Moonah's ultramodern Dickenson's Arcade, became the first venue in Tasmania with a regular floorshow. Moonah also built Australia's first open-air ice-skating rink in 1949, with a dance floor and a dais for bands, although it could not operate in warm weather, which proved rather limiting. After burning down in 1952, it was not rebuilt. By then, newer, more fashionable pursuits were in favour. In 1963, Tasmania's first ten-pin bowling centre opened to great excitement, again in Moonah, and a drive-in cinema erected in the centre of Elwick Racecourse drew crowds from all over southern Tasmania.[4]

Gwen Harwood wrote to an interstate friend in 1962:

> Last Thursday, Bill and I took the children ... to the Hobart show; we had a glorious day eating pies, chips, and the contents of sample bags while we watched the chops and the jumping; in the

Hall of Industries we saw (TRUE) a cake made in
the shape of a KOALA BEAR.[5]

The CWA ladies still proudly display their cakes
at the Royal Hobart Show, in all their various
shapes, along with jams, preserves and embroider-
ies. Sadly, they and the wood-chopping and the
Poll Herefords have been somewhat overshadowed
by newer, brighter, more technologically dazzling
things. 'There are new things to see and do which
reflect contemporary Tasmanian culture', says the
show's chief executive enthusiastically. 'Our plan
is to make the show markedly different each year
and it now bears little resemblance to what it was
a decade ago.'[6] Not everyone would see the benefit
of this. Many of the 15 000 or so people who pass
daily through the showground gates during the
last week of October are, on the contrary, seeking continuity with the past, even – or especially
– those with no direct experience of it. The show
puts them in touch with something they feel has
been lost to them. It is very reassuring that steam
tractors, fairy floss, draught horses and 'the racing
pigs, back by popular demand' can still exert their
charms in the age of YouTube and Facebook, just
as they have for generations.

Show Day holiday is important even for those who cannot be lured by the racing pigs. It is, traditionally, the day home gardeners (of which Hobart has a great many) plant out their tomato seedlings: late enough to escape the spring frosts yet early enough to ensure ripe fruit by new year.

While everyone agrees that Hobart is friendly and easygoing, it does not do fun. People do not, as a rule, spontaneously get together in public, except to fall down drunk and piss into letterboxes. There is plenty of enjoyment to be had in small groups or among friends, but you have to seek out your own kind of people. This can be a lonely place for the newcomer or the socially maladroit. Immigrants, especially those from Africa, are struck by the fact that entertainments are rarely impulsive expressions of bonhomie. 'I was used to community life where everyone interacts,' says Kiros Zegeye, who arrived from Ethiopia in 2006, 'Here, the first thing you notice is that you're not expected to socialise with your neighbours. It's the kids who first break down those barriers.'

If you like your festivities officially organised, however, you have more than enough to choose from, although you must content yourself with the knowledge that their primary aim is not to brighten your social life – that is merely a side benefit – but to promote something while making money for someone. The Antarctic Midwinter Festival has already been mentioned, but there are over thirty more, including a Kite Festival, a Mountain Festival, a Beer Festival, the Taste food festival, a Tulip Festival, a Jazz Festival, a Greek Festival, even an International Storytelling Festival. Almost all are described as 'spectacular' and 'fun for the whole family' and an alarming number involve bouncy castles, face-painting and eating. From this you might think Hobart was in a constant, never-ending state of self-pleasuring, but not many of these festivals live up to the designation. Clearly one small city cannot sustain so many, which means resources are spread very thinly. Few can ever quite dispel our awareness of some bureaucrat in an office somewhere earnestly calculating the bottom line.

Amazingly, however, people keep turning up to them, although surely they know they are being taken for a ride. One thing you can say about Hobart people is that they turn up to things. They are, on the whole, an undemanding and optimistic lot.

The Royal Hobart Regatta is the most venerable event, with the deepest roots in Hobart's social history. Along with the popular Wooden

Boat Festival, it epitomises the city's love affair with recreational sailing. In kayaks, rowboats and million-dollar yachts, Hobartians head for the Derwent in droves on weekends and holidays. Founded in 1838 by Sir John Franklin, who was homesick for the pursuits of his English youth, the regatta has been held every year since, making Regatta Day Australia's oldest public holiday. From the beginning, whaleboat races and the songs, dances and skills of the whaling crews were the main attractions, a sign that, as whaling declined in social and economic importance, the mythologising of it began. Later, races between locals and merchant navy crews took centre stage. By the early 1900s, Hobart Regatta was widely thought of as the biggest and best boating carnival in the country. Tourists from the mainland came especially to see it, at a time when visiting Tasmania was no casual undertaking.

A photograph of the 1886 event, currently in the State Archives, shows a rather demure gathering of boats and small sailing ships meandering lazily around the Derwent, with few on hand to watch: it was not an especially thrilling event, if this particular photographer is to be believed. In 1946, however, the Victory Regatta really had something to celebrate. The crowds are out in force, lining the shore and packing the jostling steam ferries. One or two men, swept up in the excitement of the moment, have even removed their hats. They are there to cheer an amateur Australian servicemen's team to victory against their British rivals in a whaleboat race, while a visiting Royal Navy warship rides disdainfully at anchor in the background.

The militarism that has always hovered in the background of this event really came to the fore in 2008 when an FI-II fighter jet performed a manoeuvre known as a 'dump and burn' over the city, spewing vast quantities of burning fuel into the sky. The shriek of the plane, the explosion of sound and the dazzling arc of white light turned dogs and cats to stone, sent plovers wheeling in panic, and no doubt caused a seizure or two at Vaucluse Gardens retirement village, but it was worth it for thirty seconds of aggro fun. A dump and burn is a long way from the simple participatory pleasures of whaleboat racing but the regatta, like the agricultural show, must 'reflect contemporary Tasmanian culture', even if nobody quite knows what that means.

Festivals these days are marketing tools, ways of packaging up disparate events and selling them to sponsors, government funding agencies and the public. This, of course, accounts for their proliferation. They are rarely genuine public commemorations of any shared historical, religious or cultural milestone. They 'celebrate' when there is nothing specifically to celebrate.

Ten Days on the Island is the state's 'official' arts festival, a biennial compendium of theatre, music, art and performance from around Australia and overseas. In essence, it is much like arts festivals everywhere, albeit on a much more modest scale. But it is its context that gives it an added frisson.

The English critic, Keith Miller, reviewing the 2008 Brighton Festival, noted that, 'As a rule these [arts festivals] take place in gracious, expansive, sturdy, slightly staid towns, whose staidness they gently try to subvert, while ensuring there's enough on the programme to keep the burghers interested. The paradigm is Edinburgh ...'[7] This provides an insight into to why *Ten Days* works as well as it does. Its bold and sporadically audacious program, while admittedly gathering into its net a large number of things that would have happened anyway, represents a real irruption of ferment into a normally rather unadventurous cultural scene. Hobart is just gracious, sturdy and staid enough to give *Ten Days* the buzz it needs to stand out.

Being government-sponsored, however, it is subject to inhibiting forces and it has to be said that, since being launched with a great flourish in 2001, its status has been allowed to wane. Government funding, never adequate, has been cut and cut again, so it is hard to see how the festival can continue to attract the signature events that give it its identity, and without which it would be reduced to nothing of real consequence. Furthermore, the government's political need to be seen to be egalitarian means that the money is spread too thinly. Instead of being concentrated in the capital, scatterings of (sometimes very minor) events are dispersed in halls and streets and cow-paddocks all over the state, thus further dissipating its energy.

These days, *Ten Days* is somewhat overshadowed by *MONA FOMA* (or, the *Museum of Old and New Art Festival of Music and Art*), an annual extravaganza of mostly rock, jazz and contemporary classical music sponsored by David Walsh and curated by Brian Ritchie. In marketing terms, *MONA FOMA* is the buzz. Its publicity, like its program, is hip and sophisticated; it generates an air of freshness, spontaneity and non-conformity; it has money enough to attract overseas artists of the calibre of P J Harvey, Pierre Henry, The Dresden Dolls and Ryoji Ikeda; and most of its sixty or more events are free and open to everyone. *MONA FOMA* is a big, classy party that takes over the city every January, rendering it almost unrecognisable. Could this really be gracious, sturdy, staid old Hobart? you wonder, as you head off to the Bahai Centre for a midnight performance of John Cage's works for prepared piano.

MONA FOMA is, of course, geared to a young audience, welcome in a city that does not offer nearly enough encouragement to its sophisticated youth. *Ten Days*, while it can dish up Taiko drummers and avant-garde Icelandic theatre, has a wider and generally more conservative constituency. The two aught to be a perfect fit.

Yet, for all its transformative influence, David Walsh's recent dramatic intervention in the cultural life of Hobart does have its dangers. The main one, of course, is that the state government, which more and more resembles an overblown accountancy practice, will be more than happy to relinquish its responsibilities for the arts to him (the Liberal opposition has signalled that it will cease funding *Ten Days* altogether if elected). Fair enough, you might say, he can obviously do it with more flair. Nevertheless, it can't be a good thing to have a state's cultural life largely in the hands of one person, however creative and generous that person might be, especially given that Walsh's wealth rests on a very fragile foundation. It would take us right back to the nineteenth-century Tory notion of culture as a gift bestowed upon a grateful populace by the rich and powerful. Unless the state government continues to shoulder its responsibilities, decision-making in the arts will cease to be a democratic and egalitarian process. Like governments everywhere, it seems to be much more interested in funding capital works, which allows it to boast about 'creating jobs' (which means 'real jobs' for real blokes in the trades), than supporting a creative society.

Walsh's contribution, in other words, must remain a welcome addition, not an alternative to public funding. The sensible response to *MONA FOMA's* success is to capitalise on it by boosting funding to *Ten Days on the Island*. The short-sighted bureaucratic response is to think, 'Oh good, he's doing it so now we don't have to.' The choice the government makes will show how much it has really learnt from the experience of MONA.

Sensory Hobart

Every city has its characteristic smells, sounds, even tastes, which change with changing circumstances. Although they rarely have the same impact as what we see, they linger in the memory, eventually coming to define a particular place for us more strongly than any of the monuments, pageants or displays devised for our benefit.

New York, for instance, is the sweet aroma of chestnuts roasting on street-corner braziers, steam rising from sidewalk gratings, the screech of subway trains, or sirens wailing through the night. Melbourne is trams rattling across intersections, cutlery clattering on footpaths under outdoor cafe tables, freshly brewed coffee in dank laneways and the clamour of Asian and European languages.

Tasmanians going to Melbourne on the overnight ferry know their destination is near when the city's polluted fug rolls across Port Phillip Bay into their cabins to awaken their noses at 6am. Like the unceasing din of traffic, it is strangely arousing, evidence of the city's energy and power.

A big city's odours and noise assert its unnaturalness. What strikes you about Hobart, on the other hand, is the refreshing absence of both. Although people living downwind of the zinc works may be sickened by its emissions, and log trucks riding their engine brakes down the southern outlet at 4am are a constant irritation to those living nearby, on the whole Hobart is peaceful, its atmosphere unencumbered.

This makes stepping out the front door for the morning paper a heady experience. The lungful of air you take in has journeyed across endless tracts of ocean and forest. It alerts you to the season: languid and sweet with pollen in summer; brisk, moist and earthy in winter. The air signals, with pinpoint accuracy, when that seemingly endless string of lazy, late-summer days suddenly crisps into autumn. There's a bracing bite to it that wasn't there yesterday. Even in the inner suburbs, you can smell the seasons.

Consequently, whatever odours there are seem

all the more potent. In the early days of settlement, the putrid stench of whale oil was so pervasive that residents agitated for a separate wharf for whaling craft further from town. A journalist writing in the *Mercury* in 1890 remembered as a boy some fifty years earlier standing in a crowd to watch a whale carcass being hauled into shallow water at Sullivans Cove to be cut up and boiled down. The smell, he said, was overpowering.[1] Fresh horse pats in the streets must also have been pungent, especially in summer, although colonial noses were no doubt as attuned to it as ours are to car exhaust, so perhaps it hardly registered. The dust constantly being thrown up from dirt roads by passing hooves and wheels did register, however, and was a major cause of complaint, since the council did not have enough water to keep it settled. So were the noxious emissions from tanners, fat-renderers, manure merchants and bone-boilers along the rivulet. Car exhausts notwithstanding, Hobart's air was a lot more noisome in the nineteenth and early twentieth centuries than it is today – more animal and more visceral – and residents had little choice but to put up with it.

Not all was stench and clatter, however. Louisa Anne Meredith delighted in the sweet perfumes of roses, sweet briar and Hawthorn in Hobart's flower gardens, which transported her back 'to the right side of the earth again'. Tasmania, in return, exported its unique botanical bouquet to the world in the form of oil extracted from native blue gums, which was widely used for soaps and inhalants.

'When you went down Kelly Steps, in the season', recalls Max Angus of his Battery Point childhood in the 1920s:

> ...the smell of raspberry jam at Peacock's Jam Factory was wonderful. The factory was slap against Kelly Steps on Salamanca Place. Further on, at the wharves opposite Parliament House, you got fishing smells, and the spicy aroma of fresh timber.

The salty, fishy smells of the waterfront and the slightly rancid pong of fishing boats at anchor have survived the area's gentrification, still evoking the romance of the sea. But this is not necessarily what fastidious outdoor diners want as they tuck into their deep-fried trevalla and freshly brewed latte. Up the hill on Hampden Road's cafe strip, the famous bakery of Jackman and McRoss fills the pre-dawn air with warm yeastiness, while the dreams of New Town and Bellerive residents,

meanwhile, are sweetened by Jean-Pascal Patisse-
ries, which, before the rest of the world is fully
awake, will be transporting the delicious aromas of
fresh breads, desserts and chocolates to specialty
food shops across the city.

In other words, Hobart's most distinctive smells
these days are not redolent of industry, labour or
export but of leisure and indulgence, reflecting a
changed economy.

Early in 2006, residents in Battery Point awoke
to an odour they found less agreeable. 'Oomph!'
coffee shop had taken to roasting beans at night,
without council permission, and the locals were up
in arms. 'It's not the smell of your freshly brewed
cup of coffee', explained resident Sandra Champion. 'This is the smell of the outer husk of the
coffee bean being burnt off and this burnt smell
goes straight out through a flue into the residential
zones of Battery Point.'[2] The spat made national
headlines because it could be exploited as a tale
of privileged folk whingeing about a minor incon-
venience. Had Chigwell residents made a similar
complaint (in the unlikely event of coffee being
roasted in Chigwell), they would not have been dismissed so readily. As it was, the critic and journalist Leo Schofield could disparage Ms Champion

and her fellow complainants as 'a little uptight, a little precious', without too much fear of contradiction. 'Get over it,' he advised. 'Part of the life and vibrancy of the city is the smells. If you take them away and deodorise the city, it ceases to be human.'[3] While this is, of course, true, it suggests an archetype of the modern city that cannot be denied, of which certain smells and noises are an inescapable part. As another Battery Point resident remarked, 'If you live in the inner city, you have to put up with that sort of thing'. It is really a question of exactly what sort of thing you're prepared to put up with and how much of it. We all have our cut-off points.

The coffee-roasting dispute aroused interest because smells are not usually subject to complaint. Noises are much more likely contenders. Those who appreciate Hobart's peacefulness are vigilant in maintaining it.

Noise Tasmania describes itself as 'an independent, non-profit, non-political body … voluntarily working towards achieving a more efficient, lawful means of reducing intrusive residential noise, thereby reducing the incidence of neighbourhood reprisals and disharmony.'[4] Its genteel desire to avoid 'neighbourhood disharmony' is reassuringly

Hobartian. Should you have need to contact Noise Tasmania, it might point you to the state government's Environment Protection Policy (Noise), which covers nuisances such as security alarms, amplified music, barking dogs (a particular problem given that there are so many dogs), traffic and aircraft noise. The relevant department provides a 24-hour hotline for complaints.

This seems unexpectedly comprehensive for a city that impresses most people as exceptionally placid. Even suburbs close to the CBD can feel eerily deserted at night, with little traffic after bedtime.

For young hormonal males, in particular, it is far too quiet, but fortunately they have hot cars to rectify the problem. Precisely because of the prevailing peacefulness, teenage hoons are more infuriating here than they are in bigger cities where their displays are swallowed up in the general din. Those anxious to draw attention to themselves by squealing their tyres have a perfect stage in the streets of suburban Hobart. Their rage against tranquillity is an enduring preoccupation of the media. Others, who are not necessarily trying to make a point, just can't afford a decent car. One Japanese tourist expressed his astonishment at the number of 'antique' Toyotas wheezing noisily up Hobart's steep hills: they are another, less flattering, economic indicator.

Peter Conrad remembers that, 'Whenever a plane spluttered over, we used to run into the streets and wave up at it, elated by this interruption of the blank blue quiet'.[5] With the airport a good way off, and commercial aircraft taking off away from the city towards the mainland, the sound of planes is still a rarity, apart from the annoying buzz of Cessnas taking tourists on joy flights. Hobart's skies are quieter than those of any other capital. This is, of course, a blessing, although it reinforces the feeling of being at the end of the line.

The urgent, eerie ack-ack-ack of plovers hurrying to wherever it is plovers go in the middle of the night, and the three low, booming blasts from a departing cruise ship rounding up its flock (on summer evenings only, and always dead on 6pm): these are among Hobart's most characteristic and evocative modern sounds. They can hardly be called a nuisance because they do not suggest a lack of consideration on anyone's part.

Church bells might suggest just that, however, at least to those who, ignoring history, piously reject the 'privileging' of Christianity. Not that church bells are exclusive to Hobart, of course, but their clarity on a calm Sunday morning as they echo off the surrounding hillsides gives them a particular resonance. For those of a nostalgic temperament, they confirm Hobart's respectability and its English heritage.

At the beginning of the nineteenth century, following a period of widespread atheism in France, Chateaubriand wrote of the particular impact of church bells and their ability to touch the hearts even of non-believers in a way that no other sound can, especially after a long silence. He was pointing to the importance in our lives of the mythic and non-rational.

Two hundred years later, towards the end of 2007, after structural failure had forced the closure of Holy Trinity Church in North Hobart the majority of residents found that they, too, missed its calls to worship, even those who had never heeded them in the past. Holy Trinity has the oldest peal of bells of its type outside England. It is one of only two in Tasmania (the other being at St David's Cathedral) hung to swing full-circle for change ringing: an orderly sequence of tuned bells producing a cascade of sound without any recognisable tune. It is unmistakeably English, presenting the Greek Orthodox Church, which has now taken possession of Holy Trinity, with an interesting denominational dilemma.

In a storeroom behind the church lies a small wooden frame, discoloured with age, that was sent from London in 1847 to guide local carpenters in the construction of a full-sized support for the three tons of bells in the tower. It was all very well for Holy Trinity to have purchased an expensive new peal of eight bells but, as was so often the case in the nineteenth century, ambition outstripped capability (the opposite being generally true today), for the little colony had no bell-hanger. Although local tradesmen managed to replicate the frame and hoist it laboriously into position, the green wood they used warped, which meant ringing had to be abandoned in the late 1960s.

John Smith was among a band of enthusiasts who secured a Commonwealth bicentennial grant to return the bells to London for rehanging on a steel frame. In 1987, he was among those who pulled the bell ropes again for the first time in nearly two decades.

'St David's bells are better than Trinity's for tone and quality of sound,' he admits, 'because the technology had improved by 1936 when the ones at

St David's were cast. They are very good and there are ten of them, which is an unusual number.' The problem, however, is the blank wall of the high-rise building just down the road. 'It causes an echo which makes the bells sound awful, especially when you're driving down Macquarie Street. Holy Trinity's bells sound much clearer because there are no obstructions.'

Why ring bells? 'Well, you have to be a bit of a nerd', he jokes.

> It's pointless really. What matters is enthusiasm.
> You do it because the sound is beautiful and
> because you're marking important community
> events such as weddings and funerals. And it's
> also wonderful to be part of an international
> fellowship of bellringers. We had people come
> from all over the world to ring at Holy Trinity. It's
> called 'tower grabbing': travelling around, ringing
> in as many different churches as possible. It's quite
> competitive. International tours are organised.

Teenagers, he says, are quickest to master change ringing because they have both the mental co-ordination and the physical energy. Sadly, though, few are interested.

John, speaking before its fate was decided,

when demolition was still very much on the cards, remained sanguine about the closure of the church.

> It doesn't mean much to the average person, and those who do care are concerned about the building itself: the heritage rather than the religious side. The biggest loss is that people won't hear the bells any more. There were a couple of serial complainers, but most people enjoyed the sound.

Given that Hobart prides itself on the quality of its produce and its restaurants, the results of a visitor survey taken in 2008 by the Department of Primary Industries must have come as quite a shock. No wonder the state government released them only after a Freedom of Information application. Respondents complained that eating out in Tasmania was a hit and miss affair: restaurants were too expensive, they said, the presentation was old fashioned and the food itself of variable quality. Particularly wounding was that none of them included food or wine among their reasons for coming.

The head of Brand Tasmania, Robert Heazle-wood, not surprisingly, dismissed the survey as 'blatantly wrong'. Richard Bovill, organiser of the Fair Dinkum Foods campaign, lamented that tourists were 'not hearing our message'.[6] It could be, of course, that they were hearing it perfectly well but disagreeing with it, although in the wonderful world of PR that possibility is never an option. Whether reliably or not, the survey suggested that, while Tasmanian salmon, oysters, truffles and wines are highly regarded interstate and overseas, perhaps too little attention had been given to their presentation at home.

As restaurant critic Graeme Phillips sensibly pointed out, however:

> The problem for Tasmania is that, unlike tourists to other states who, for example, hit Adelaide and the Barossa and say they've done SA, most visitors here tour the whole island and so get a disproportionate share of our hits and misses.[7]

Much has changed since the survey was carried out, and today the results would surely be very different. A number of informal, bistro-style restaurants, serving imaginatively prepared local seasonal produce, are leading the way from stuffiness to chic.

The most hyped is Garagistes in Murray Street, with its fashionable no-bookings policy, its big shared tables and a constantly changing selection of organic food and wines. Choose from such delicacies as fried pigs' ears, fermented turnip stems, salsify, sorrel or sea urchin, but be prepared to wait hungrily for a seat, especially in summer. It is not uncommon for interstate visitors to fly in to Hobart for MONA and dinner at Garagistes before flying straight out again, which tends to make tourism officials rather cross. Ethos Eat Drink, in a converted 1820s stable in Elizabeth Street, serves a succession of small tapas-style dishes, priding itself on its biodynamic vegetables and hand-reared and 'ethically-killed' meat and fish (for which the creatures concerned are surely grateful). The plates have been custom-made by a local potter, and even the soaps in the bathrooms are 'artisan'.

In tandem, a lively Sunday farmers' market has sprung up on an empty lot in Elizabeth Street, just up the road from Ethos, along with some smart new food shops. Hobartians have long enjoyed a range of high-quality delis and corner shops, among them Lipscombe Larder in Sandy Bay, The Salad Bowl in West Hobart, the various Hill Street Stores, The Foodstore in Lenah Valley and the irresistible Wursthaus at Salamanca, which has fresh Tasmanian truffles in late winter, and cheeses and prepared meats in almost shameful abundance. These old acquaintances have recently been joined by a pack of glamorous newcomers: the Italian Pantry and Bottega Rotolo for all things Mediterranean, Matthew Evans's tiny A Common Ground, which is tucked under a staircase off Salamanca Place, Jam Packed, and several others. The big supermarkets are insufferably bland and joyless by comparison.

There are dozens of foods that say 'Tassie': leatherwood honey; fish, of which there are many peculiar to this state; abalone; fresh oysters, available almost all year round; wallaby and emu; locally grown wasabi; walnuts; truffles; potatoes, of which there are varieties grown and eaten only in Tasmania; fancy lettuces – one farm at Cambridge, not far from Hobart airport, producing fifteen different sorts; fresh local shitake and oyster mushrooms, which you can buy cheaply in almost any fruit and vegie shop; berries; crayfish; anchovies and kelp.

'There's also a long tradition of hunting wild game in this state', says food writer Bernard Lloyd:

> More so than elsewhere in Australia. And we
> have the shack tradition [self-built seaside or

bush shacks on government land, where people spent their weekends and holidays], all of which encouraged the appreciation of simple, natural foods … Tasmanians grow a lot of their own fruits and vegetables, we have the highest percentage of boat owners in the country, and we can still pluck fresh oysters off the rocks. Also, there's not a big divide between the country and the city. Proportionately, because it's a small community, the influence of niche-market producers is much greater. That means we know about fresh foods, so restaurants have a knowledgeable clientele, even though it may not always be a sophisticated one.

Cafe culture is to literary life as pub culture is to contemporary popular music. This is why conservatives often sneer at 'latte sippers', because they understand the insidious link between coffee shops and intellectualism: a connection that goes all the way back to the coffee houses of eighteenth-century London, which were the incubators of the modern sensibility.

Hence, people tend to identify the opening of certain cafes as marking important stages in social advancement. They served as the colonising spaces of civil behaviour. 'I remember the excitement of the first cafes opening,' writes Dennis Altman of his student years in the 1950s, 'complete with cappuccino machines and exotic dishes such as "Russian egg salad".'[8] He doesn't name any of them, which is unusual, for their names were of vital importance. Peter Conrad remembers the Brazil in Sandy Bay, the headquarters of 'our local unkempt Bohemia',[9] and, in 1994, Gwen Harwood noted, 'We are going with friends to the Ali Akbar which is beginning to assume the part of the Cafe Royal (should that be Royale?) in Hobart's literary life.'[10] It is significant that these places bore exotic foreign names that hinted at escape.

'Hobart gets the new coffee habit', announced the *Mercury* in February 1956. With the opening of the Manhattan Coffee Lounge in Murray Street, 'Hobart has entered the era of the Espresso Coffee Shop – the espresso which originated in Italy a generation ago and recently took London and Paris by storm ... every cup is made to order.'[11] The Manhattan's sleek, cosmopolitan modernity – its very un-Hobartness – was boldly announced by a Max

Angus mural on the back wall showing glittering New York skyscrapers under a smiling sun. 'The Manhattan was a roaring success,' says founder Eric Hayes. 'We were jam-packed from day one. We had up to fourteen people working behind the counter; the place was clean and new, the staff were dressed in white jackets and aprons, and it was trendy – the fashionable place to go.'[12]

Smart and new are not necessarily the defining features of trendiness today. With cafes and coffee shops of every description on almost every street corner, the discerning – those who want to set themselves apart from the herd – choose to drink their coffee at places with a story. The Retro, the first cafe at Salamanca, has plenty of stories and, as a consequence, the aura of authenticity that keeps its customers loyal.

'A friend of ours opened an art gallery at Salamanca in the late 1970s', recalls Chris Pearce:

> ...but he was all alone. He said he could have
> bought all these old warehouses for $64 000 then.
> There was a junk shop but other than that the
> buildings were entirely dilapidated. When I was
> young we never came down here at all. You'd go to
> the wharves to buy fish but you'd avoid Salamanca

Place. The Retro was the first cafe in the area.
That and the Saturday morning market started
the gentrification.

Those in the know insist that the Retro's coffee
is unsurpassed, but that is not really the point. It
is no accident that, when the *New York Times* ran a
travel feature on Hobart in 2007, it began with
this unremarkable little establishment:

> It's Friday afternoon in the Tasmanian capital,
> Hobart, and the crowd at Retro, a harborside cafe
> adorned with free-form mosaic art, is decidedly
> offbeat. A fleece-clad couple sip lattes and a
> spiky-haired musician carrying a guitar case greets
> a friend. A cyclist in spandex pedals by so slowly
> that his wheels barely move.[13]

And so on.

What this agglomeration of journalistic clichés adds up to is an image of a coffee shop as the
embodiment of the city's character, or at least the
way certain elements would like it to be. The *New
York Times'* headline – 'Tasmania Goes Boutique:
Nice and Slow' – pretty well sums up Hobart's
contemporary aspirations, both official and unof-
ficial, although not necessarily its actual practices.

Today, being fastidious about the quality of your short black or macchiato marks you out as worldly and sophisticated. But this is a ruse. It is not the brew people are seeking so much as the company of like-minded people and the quality of their conversations. The extraordinary proliferation of cafes and coffee shops has created the conditions for civilised discourse in a city that provides few other opportunities.

And it is civilised discourse, promoted by immigrants from interstate and overseas, a healthy economy and modern communication technologies, that has helped to banish Hobart's insularity, making it more creative, expansive, confident and *civilised*. Nobody would call a coffee shop 'the Manhattan' today, unless they intended irony.

In every cafe and restaurant, all across town, conversations will eventually turn to the question of what Hobart is and what it might become. People here are vitally interested in — and anxious about — their city, which is still manageable enough for them to feel *is* their city, but which they worry may be starting to slip out of their control. There is despair at modernising changes that point in the wrong direction and a wealth of divergent opinion about what the right direction might be. The anxiety underlying all these conversations is about how Hobart can adapt to change while remaining Hobart: how the city can maintain its special character – however that might be perceived – as it expands and develops.

Hobart's great paradox is that most of what people admire about it today is a result of poverty in the past. Its Georgian buildings survive because nobody could afford to replace them, for example; its population is manageable because so many people have had to seek work elsewhere; its natural surroundings have been preserved because building high on the hillsides was, financially, out of the question. How much of that character will have to be sacrificed now that poverty is no longer the determining factor?

There are those of little confidence who still believe that 'the source of all cultural value and human ingenuity ... lies elsewhere', as the Tasmanian writer, Peter Hay, claims, who yearn for Hobart to be 'just as good as' Melbourne and Sydney, and who see economic prosperity as an end in itself. Sadly, at present, they tend to be the ones with power and influence. Yet, at the same time, there is an increasing number who know and respect the city's rich history, who love the place for what it is and want to preserve its most endearing qualities. They are happy to envisage Hobart as 'going boutique, nice and slow'. Often they are blow-ins from the mainland or from overseas who have lived in large, impersonal cities and see qualities in Hobart that the locals have not always been in a position to appreciate.

A modernising vision — centralist, purposeful, hierarchical, driven by economics and always looking over its shoulder — is pitched against what might be called a postmodernising one, more concerned with difference, participation and the uncompetitive pleasures of a regional outlook. The one is hard, thrusting and no-nonsense, the other flexible, accommodating and, as it happens, more attuned to a post-industrial world.

You have only to sit down over a bottle of wine with a group of long-term residents and listen to their stories of the past — even the fairly recent past — to realise the remarkable social, technological and economic transformation that has overtaken this city. They may, of course, be nostalgic — people very often are — and quick to complain about what has been lost. Yet you will see a confidence there too, a growing feeling of optimism and self-assuredness. As Simon Barcza puts it, 'Hobart is definitely on the up-and-up. There's more activity at nights, people are more involved than ever in the arts and community activities.' John Smith sees that 'people are less introverted, more open and friendly now than they were even a couple of decades ago.' And, when asked what he thought of Hobart today, the 94-year-old Max Angus declared exuberantly, 'It's absolutely marvellous. There's so much going on here now, I never would have thought it possible. What a place to be!'

Notes

The fabric of the city

1 *Mercury*, 10 June 1938, p. 10.
2 L Woolley, 'Urban Nature and City Design', in *Island*, no 84, p. 9.
3 Quoted in J Boyce, *Van Dieman's Land*, p. 123.
4 Quoted in F Bolt, *The Founding of Hobart: a Diary Recounting the Events on the Derwent 1803–1804*, p. 86.
5 S Petrow & A Alexander, *Growing with Strength: a History of the Hobart City Council, 1846–2000*, p. 32.
6 Quoted in P Bolger, *Hobart Town*, p. 55.
7 Quoted in S Petrow, 'Servicing the City', in K Evans & I Terry, *Living and Working in Hobart: Historical Perspectives. Papers and Proceedings of the Conference held by the Professional Historians Association (Tasmania) on 30 October 2002*, p. 52.
8 A Alexander, *Glenorchy 1804–1964*, p. 105.
9 L Woolley, 'Urban Nature and City Design'.
10 R Atkinson, R Dufty & L Pichot, *Missed Opportunities: an Appraisal of Hobart's CBD*, p. 5.
11 *Mercury*, 13 November 2007, p. 23.
12 D Altman, *Defying Gravity, a Political Life*, p. 11.
13 *Sunday Tasmanian*, 7 September 2008, p. 19.
14 Hobart City Council, submission to Productivity Commission Public Enquiry, *Conservation of Australia's Historic Heritage Places*, p. 1.
15 Quoted on the Tasmanian Government's website for the

Hobart Waterfront International Design Competition, viewed 20 October 2008, <www.hwidc.tas.gov.au>.

16 B Shelton, 'This is not a Suburb', in *Island*, no. 40, p. 45.

Further afield

1 A Alexander (ed.), *The Companion to Tasmanian History*, p. 184, and A Alexander, *Glenorchy 1804–1964*, p. 289.

2 J Attlee, *Isolarion*, p. 87.

3 Hobart City Council, *Battery Point Planning Scheme*, p. 9.

4 *Tasmanian Times*, 29 October 2006.

5 Hobart City Council, *Battery Point Planning Scheme*, p. 9.

As seen from afar

1 Quoted in G Williams and A Frost, *Terra Australis to Australia*, p. 103.

2 P Bolger, *Hobart Town*, p. 44.

3 Quoted in K Harman, *Australia Brought to Book: Responses to Australia by Visiting Writers 1836–1939*, p. 155.

4 K Harman, *Australia Brought to Book*, p. 184.

5 Quoted in G Kratzmann (ed.), *A Steady Storm of Correspondence: Selected Letters of Gwen Harwood 1943–1995*, p. 289.

6 L Simpson, 'Tom Gilling and Heather Rose', in *Island*, no. 82, p. 81.

7 G Young, 'Isle of Gothic Silence', in *Island*, no. 60–61, pp. 31–32.

8 D Altman, *Defying Gravity*, p. 20.

9 L McGaurr, *Lonely Planet Guide: Tasmania*, p. 123.

10 *Sunday Tasmanian*, 23 November 2008, p. 22.

11 Quoted in G Kratzmann (ed.) *A Steady Storm of Correspondence*, p. 79.

12 J Flanagan, *Dropped from the Moon: the Settlement Experiences of Refugee Communities in Tasmania*, p. 30–31.

13 J Boyce, *Van Diemen's Land*, p. 25.

14 J Cassidy, 'Migration', in A Alexander (ed.), *The Companion to Tasmanian History*, p. 237.

Buying and selling

1   M Nash, *The Bay Whalers: Tasmania's Shore-Based Whaling Industry*,
    p. 115.
2   M Nash, *The Bay Whalers*, p. 115.
3   P Bolger, *Hobart Town*, p. 196.
4   Hydro-Electric Commission, 'Report for the Year 1929–
    1930', quoted in FK Crowley, *Modern Australia in Documents*, vol.
    I, p. 408.
5   S Alomes, 'Treasures of the Mind', in *Island*, no. 8, p. 18.
6   P Hay, *Vandiemonian Essays*, p. 126.
7   All my figures on gambling are taken from South Australian
    Centre for Economic Studies, *Social and Economic Impact Study into
    Gambling in Tasmania.*
8   V Smith, 'Growing up in Hobart', in *Island*, no. 34–35, pp.12–19.
9   *Mercury*, 14 November 2008, p. 10.
10 Hobart City Council, Welcome to Salamanca Market,
    viewed 10 February 2008, <www.hobartcity.com.au/HCC/
    STANDARD/SALAMANCA_MARKET.html>.
11 *Salamanca Market Sustainability Study*, prepared for Hobart City
    Council, 2007, p. 2.

The prison becomes a salon

1   P Conrad, *Down Home: Revisiting Tasmania*, p. 25.
2   CJ Koch, *The Boys in the Island*, p. 8.
3   D Altman, *Defying Gravity*, p. 12.
4   S Harrex, 'Island Lyrics', in *Island*, no 25–6, p. 68.
5   V Smith, 'Growing up in Hobart', in *Island*, no. 34–5, p. 4.
6   A Trollope, *Victoria and Tasmania*, p. 154.
7   J Boyce, *Van Diemen's Land*, p. 250.
8   *Mercury*, 19 September 1988, p. 9.
9   L Broughton, *A Place for Art: a Century of Art, Craft, Design and
    Industrial Arts Education in Hobart*, p. 68.
10 Reproduced in FK Crowley, *Modern Australia in Documents*,
    vol. 2, p. 558.

Doberman or labrador

1   A Alexander, *Glenorchy 1804–1964*, p. 113.
2   *Mercury*, 2 May 1938, p. 1.
3   *Mercury*, 6 May 1963, p. 4.
4   M Scott, 'Changing Countries', in *Island*, no. 52, p. 13.
5   *The Australian*, 'Travel and Indulgence', 26–27 April 2008, p. 3.

A succession of pasts

1   M de Kretser, *The Lost Dog*, p. 93.
2   P Hay, *Vandiemonian Essays*, p. ix.
3   J Boyce, *Van Diemen's Land*, p. 317.
4   J Boyce, *Van Diemen's Land*, p. 225.
5   P Bolger, *Hobart Town*, p. 94.
6   D Young, *Making Crime Pay: the Evolution of Convict Tourism in Tasmania*, p. 33.
7   M Scott, *Port Arthur: a Story of Strength and Courage*, p. 6.
8   M Scott, *Port Arthur*, p. 15.
9   A Trollope, *Victoria and Tasmania*, p. 163.
10 V Smith, 'Growing up in Hobart', in *Island* no. 34–5, pp. 12–19.
11 A Nicolson, *Sissinghurst: an Unfinished History*, p. 36.
12 P Conrad, *Down Home*, p. 107.

Nature within cooee

1   LA Meredith, *My Home in Tasmania*, p. 24.
2   P Conrad, *Down Home*, p. 30.
3   M Lawrence, *The Mountain*, DVD.
4   H Reynolds, 'The Pigeon House', in *Island*, no. 100, pp. 18–19.
5   EM Christensen & MC Jones, *Before They Built the Bridge: an Anecdotal History*, p. 85.
6   M Mulligan & S Hill, *Ecological Pioneers: a Social History of Australian Ecological Thought and Action*, p. 243.

7   Quoted in T Bonyhady, *The Colonial Earth*, p. 90.

8   D Altmann, *Defying Gravity*, p. 23.

9   Quoted in B Beale, *If Trees Could Speak: Stories of Australia's Greatest Trees*, p. 109.

10 G Sheridan, 'Mystery and Malevolence: the Royal Tasmanian Botanical Gardens celebrates 190 years', in *Fagus, the Magazine of Friends of the Royal Tasmanian Botanical Gardens*, November 2008.

11 S Hannaford, *Walch's Hand-book of Garden and Greenhouse Culture in Tasmania*, p. 136.

12 H Reynolds, 'The Pigeon House', in *Island*, no. 100, p. 20.

13 R McNeice, 'Bushfires', in A Alexander (ed.), *The Companion to Tasmanian History*, p. 59.

14 G Kratzmann (ed.), *A Steady Storm of Correspondence*, p. 210.

15 T Bowden, 'Tasmania – the Testicle of Australia', paper presented at the In the First Person conference, 2008.

16 M Tattersall, web blog, viewed 5 January 2009, <www.members.iinet.net.au/~mtattersall/Articles/Forestry.htm>.

17 *Mercury*, 14 March 2009, p. 9.

18 I am grateful to Anne Parker for this information.

'Cool off in Tasmania'

1   Charles Darwin and Jessie Couvreur are quoted on the website Wellington Park Management Trust, Written Interpretations, viewed 20 November 2008, <www.wellingtonpark.tas.gov.au/pdf/writtenInterpretation.pdf>.

2   A Trollope, *Victoria and Tasmania*, p. 160.

3   T Bowden, 'Tasmania – the Testicle of Australia'.

4   Quoted in F Bolt, *The Founding of Hobart*, p. 209.

5   Quoted in N Shakespeare, *In Tasmania*, p. 228.

6   A Trollope, *Victoria and Tasmania*, p. 160.

7   A Alexander, *Glenorchy 1804–1964*, p. 16.

8   J Flanagan, *Dropped from the Moon*, pp. 32–33.

9   *Mercury*, 6 May 1963, p. 4.

10 *Sunday Tasmanian*, 10 February 2008, p. 25.

Bad behaviour

1 A Alexander (ed.), *The Companion to Tasmanian History*, p. 91.
2 Quoted in S Lawrence, *Whalers and Free Men: Life on Tasmania's Colonial Whaling Stations*, p. 28.
3 S Lawrence, *Whalers and Free Men*, pp. 21–22.
4 LA Meredith, *My Home in Tasmania*, p. 36.
5 P Bolger, *Hobart Town*, p. 31.
6 Quoted in P Bolger, *Hobart Town*, p. 36.
7 D Young, *Making Crime Pay*, p. 48.
8 A Alexander (ed.), *The Companion to Tasmanian History*, p. 91.
9 *Mercury*, 15 May 1963, p. 13.
10 J Flanagan, *Dropped from the Moon*, p. 49.
11 J Flanagan, *Dropped from the Moon*, p. 49–50.
12 *Mercury*, 2 November 2007, p. 6.
13 *Mercury*, 7 November 2007, p. 9.
14 *Mercury*, 26 September 1988, p. 8.

Keeping occupied

1 *Mercury*, 19 December 2005, p. 14.
2 J Boyce, *Van Diemen's Land*, p. 137.
3 A Hume, quoted in R Ely, 'Larrikins, Brawlers and Troublemakers in Hobart Town', in K Evans and I Terry, *Living and Working in Hobart*, p. 69.
4 This information taken from A Alexander, *Glenorchy 1804–1964*.
5 G Kratzmann (ed.), *A Steady Storm of Correspondence*, p. 169.
6 *The Australian*, 15 October 2006.
7 *Times Literary Supplement*, 30 May 2008, p. 17.

Sensory Hobart

1 P Bolger, *Hobart Town*, p. 77.
2 *PM*, ABC Radio National, 1 February 2006.
3 *PM*, ABC Radio National, 1 February 2006.
4 Department of Primary Industries, Water and Environment,

Noise Tasmania, Our Objectives, viewed 5 March 2009, <www.au.geocities.com/noisetas/objectives.html>.

5   P Conrad, *Down Home*, p. 137.

6   *Mercury*, 25 March 2008, pp. I & 2.

7   *Sunday Tasmanian*, 30 March 2008, p. 16.

8   D Altman, *Defying Gravity*, p. II.

9   P Conrad, *Down Home*, p. 28.

10 G Kratzmann (ed.), *A Steady Storm of Correspondence*, p. 459.

11 *Mercury*, 4 February 1956, p. 4.

12 Quoted in P County & B Lloyd, *Before We Eat: a Delicious Slice of Tasmania's Culinary Life*, p. 186.

13 *New York Times*, 29 July 2007.

Bibliography

Periodicals and websites

Department of Primary Industries, Water and Environment,
  Noise Tasmania, Our Objectives, viewed 5 March 2009,
  <www.au.geocities.com/noisetas/objectives.html>.

Hobart City Council, Welcome to Salamanca Market, viewed
  10 February 2008, <www.hobartcity.com.au/HCC/
  STANDARD/SALAMANCA_MARKET.html>.

Island, no. 6, 1981 – no. 114, 2008.

Mercury, various issues.

Sauce: music/fashion/digital life/film/comedy/arts, various issues.

Sunday Tasmanian, various issues.

Tasmanian Government, Hobart Waterfront International Design
  Competition, viewed 20 October 2008, <www.hwidc.tas.gov.au>.

Tasmanian Life, various issues.

Tasmanian Review, no. 1, 1979 – no. 5, 1980.

Tattersall, M, web blog, viewed 5 January 2009, <www.members.
  iinet.net.au/~mtattersall/Articles/Forestry.htm>.

Wellington Park Management Trust, Written Interpretations,
  viewed 20 November 2008, <www.wellingtonpark.tas.gov.au/
  pdf/writtenInterpretation.pdf>.

Books and other publications

Alexander, A, *Glenorchy 1804–1964*, Glenorchy City Council,
  Hobart, 1986.

—— (ed.), *The Companion to Tasmanian History*, Centre for Tasmanian Historical Studies, University of Tasmania, Hobart, 2005.

Alomes, S, 'Treasures of the Mind', in *Island*, no. 8, 1981.

Altman, D, *Defying Gravity, a Political Life*, Allen & Unwin, Melbourne, 1997.

Atkinson, R, Dufty, R & Pichot, L, *Missed Opportunities: an Appraisal of Hobart's CBD*, Housing and Community Research Unit, University of Tasmania, Hobart, 2007.

Attlee, J, *Isolarion: a Different Oxford Journey*, University of Chicago Press, Chicago, 2007.

Australian Bureau of Statistics, *Census of Population and Housing: Selected Characteristics for Urban Centres, Australia, 2001*, Commonwealth of Australia, Canberra, 2003.

Barrett, C, *Isle of Mountains: Roaming through Tasmania*, Cassell and Company Ltd, Melbourne, 1946.

Beale, B, *If Trees Could Speak: Stories of Australia's Greatest Trees*, Allen & Unwin, Melbourne, 2007.

Bolger, P, *Hobart Town*, Australian National University Press, Canberra, 1973.

Bolt, F, *The Founding of Hobart: a Diary Recounting the Events on the Derwent 1803–1804*, Peregrine Publishing, Kettering, Tasmania, 2004.

Bonyhady, T, *The Colonial Earth*, Miegunyah Press, Melbourne, 2000.

Bowden, T, 'Tasmania – the Testicle of Australia', paper presented at the In the First Person conference, National Library of Australia, 10–11 May 2008.

Boyce, J, *Van Diemen's Land*, Black Inc, Melbourne, 2008.

Broughton, L, *A Place for Art: a Century of Art, Craft, Design and Industrial Arts Education in Hobart*, University of Tasmania, Centre for the Arts in conjunction with Hobart Technical College, Hobart, 1988.

Brown, B, *I Excel: the Life and Times of Sir Henry Jones*, Libra, Hobart, 1991.

Bibliography

Cannon, M, *Australia in the Victorian Age, Volume 3: Life in the Cities*, Thomas Nelson, Melbourne, 1976.

Christensen, EM & Jones, MC, *Before They Built the Bridge: an Anecdotal History*, Elizabeth Christensen, Hobart, 1997.

Collier, P, *Wildflowers of Mount Wellington*, Society for Growing Native Plants, Tasmanian Region Inc, Hobart, 1988.

Community Development Division, Hobart City Council, *Salamanca Market Stallholders' Guide*, Hobart City Council, 2004.

Conrad, P, *Down Home: Revisiting Tasmania*, Chatto & Windus, London, 1988.

County, P & Lloyd, B, *Before We Eat: a Delicious Slice of Tasmania's Culinary Life*, The Culinary Historians of Tasmania, Hobart, 2003.

Crowley, FK, *Modern Australia in Documents*, Wren, Melbourne, 1973.

Davenport, WT & City of Clarence Council, *Spirit of Clarence: a Tasmanian Community*, City of Clarence, Hobart, 1989.

de Kretser, M, *The Lost Dog*, Allen & Unwin, Sydney, 2007.

Eldridge, M, 'New Mountain, New River, New Home? The Hmong in Tasmania', MA thesis, University of Tasmania, 2008.

Enterprise Marketing and Research Services Pty Ltd, *Salamanca Market Sustainability Study*, Hobart City Council, 2007.

Evans, K & Terry, I (eds), *Living and Working in Hobart: Historical Perspectives. Papers and Proceedings of the Conference held by the Professional Historians Association (Tasmania) on 30 October 2002*, Professional Historians Association (Tasmania), Hobart, 2003.

Flanagan, J, *Dropped from the Moon: the Settlement Experiences of Refugee Communities in Tasmania*, Social Action and Research Centre, Anglicare, Hobart, 2007.

Flanagan, M, *In Sunshine or in Shadow*, Picador, Sydney, 2002.

Hannaford, S, *Walch's Hand-book of Garden and Greenhouse Culture in Tasmania*, 2nd edn, J Walch, Hobart, 1884.

Harman, K, *Australia Brought to Book: Responses to Australia by Visiting*

Writers 1836–1939, Boobook, Sydney, 1985.

Harrex, S, 'Island Lyrics', in *Island*, no. 25–6, 1986.

Hay, P, *Vandiemonian Essays*, Walleah Press, Hobart, 2002.

Henricksen, N, *Island and Otherland: Christopher Koch and his Books*, Educare, Melbourne, 2003.

Hobart City Council, *Battery Point Planning Scheme*, Hobart City Council, 1979.

—— *City of Hobart Planning Scheme*, Hobart City Council, 1982.

—— Submission to Productivity Commission Public Enquiry, *Conservation of Australia's Historic Heritage Places*, July 2005.

—— *Hobart City Council Annual Report, 2006/2007*, Hobart City Council, 2007.

Hughes, R, *The Fatal Shore*, Pan Books, London, 1988.

Johnston, RM, *Tasmanian Official Record 1892*, Government Printer, Hobart, 1892.

Koch, CJ, *The Boys in the Island*, Angus & Robertson, Sydney, 1987.

Kratzmann, G (ed.), *A Steady Storm of Correspondence: Selected Letters of Gwen Harwood 1943–1995*, University of Queensland Press, Brisbane, 2001.

Lawrence, M, *The Mountain*, DVD, Thunderbolt Productions, Hobart, 2007.

Lawrence, S, *Whalers and Free Men: Life on Tasmania's Colonial Whaling Stations*, Australian Scholarly Publishing, Melbourne, 2006.

Lewis, N & Aitken, R, *Government House, Hobart: Garden and Grounds Conservation Analysis and Conservation Policies*, unpublished report, in possession of Government House, Hobart, 1991.

Lohrey, A, *The Morality of Gentlemen*, Montpelier Press, Hobart, 2002.

McCooey, D, 'In dialogue with Vivian Smith', *Dialogues with Poets*, issue 5, Summer 2003.

McGaurr, L, *Lonely Planet Guide: Tasmania*, Lonely Planet Publications, Melbourne, 1999.

Meredith, LA, *My Home in Tasmania*, (facsimile edition of original published in 1852), Glamorgan Spring Bay Historical Society, Swansea, Tasmania, 2003.

Bibliography

Miley, C, *Beautiful and Useful: the Arts and Crafts Movement in Tasmania*, Queen Victoria Museum and Art Gallery, Launceston, 1987.

Mulligan, M & Hill, S, *Ecological Pioneers: a Social History of Australian Ecological Thought and Action*, Cambridge University Press, UK, 2001.

Nash, M, *The Bay Whalers: Tasmania's Shore-Based Whaling Industry*, Navarine Publishing, Canberra, 2003.

Nicolson, A, *Sissinghurst: an Unfinished History*, Harper Collins, London, 2008.

Petrow, S & Alexander, A, *Growing with Strength: a History of the Hobart City Council, 1846–2000*, Hobart City Council, 2008.

Rayner, T, 'Hobart', in P Beilharz & T Hogan, *Sociology: Place, Time and Division*, Oxford University Press, Melbourne, 2006.

Reynolds, H, 'The Pigeon House', in *Island*, no. 100, 2005.

Ross, J (ed.), *Chronicle of Australia*, Chronicle Australasia Pty Ltd, Melbourne, 1993.

Rowntree, A & Rowntree, F, *Early Settlement of Sandy Bay*, Mercury Press, Hobart, 1959.

Ryan, L, *The Aboriginal Tasmanians*, Allen & Unwin, Melbourne, 1996.

Scott, M, 'Changing Countries', in *Island*, no. 52, 1992.

—— *Port Arthur: a Story of Strength and Courage*, Random House, Sydney, 1997.

Shakespeare, N, *In Tasmania*, Random House, Sydney, 2004.

Shelton, B, 'This is not a Suburb', in *Island*, no. 40, 1989.

Sheridan, G, 'Mystery and Malevolence: the Royal Tasmanian Botanical Gardens celebrates 190 years', (reprinted from Australian Garden History, vol. 20, no. 2) in *Fagus, the Magazine of Friends of the Royal Tasmanian Botanical Gardens*, November 2008.

Simpson, L, 'Tom Gilling and Heather Rose', in *Island*, no. 82, 2000.

Smith, V, 'Growing up in Hobart', in *Island*, no. 34–5, 1988.

South Australian Centre for Economic Studies, *Social and Economic Impact Study into Gambling in Tasmania, vol. 1, Final Report*,

Department of Treasury and Finance, Government of Tasmania, June 2008.

Tardif, P, *John Bowen's Hobart: the Beginning of European Settlement in Tasmania*, Tasmanian Historical Research Association, Hobart, 2003.

Ten Days on the Island programme, Roar Film, Hobart 2009.

Terry, I & Austral Archaeology, *Historical Overview of Queens Domain Hobart*, Hobart City Council, 1999.

Thorp, V, *Derwent River Wildlife Guide*, Tasmanian Environment Centre Inc, Hobart, 2000.

Trollope, A, *Victoria and Tasmania*, Kessinger Publishing, n.d. (facsimile edn of 'Victoria & Tasmania' in A Trollope, *Australia and New Zealand*, Chapman & Hall, London, 1874).

Welcome to Hobart: Official Visitors' Guide to Hobart and Surrounds, Vibe Tasmania Official Visitors' Guides, Hobart, 2008.

Williams, G & Frost, A, *Terra Australis to Australia*, Oxford University Press, Melbourne, 1988.

Winter, G (ed.), *Tasmanian Insights: Essays in Honour of Geoffrey Thomas Stilwell*, State Library of Tasmania, Hobart, 1992.

Wooley, C & Tatlow, M, *A Walk in Old Hobart*, Walk Guides Australia, Tasmania, 2007.

Woolley, L, 'Urban Nature and City Design', in *Island*, no. 84, 2000–2001.

Young, D, *Making Crime Pay: the Evolution of Convict Tourism in Tasmania*, Tasmanian Historical Research Association, Hobart, 1996.

Young, G, 'Isle of Gothic Silence', in *Island*, no. 60–61, 1994.

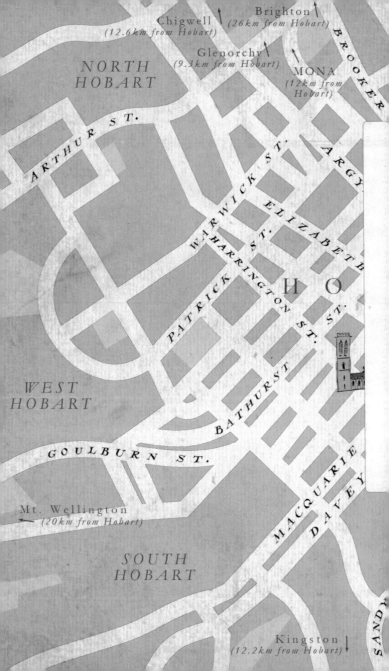